WINDOWS 11 FOR

SENIORS

Unlock the Simplicity! Master Your Computer with Easy Steps, Helpful Tips, and Clear Illustrations

Marlon French

TABLE OF CONTENTS

TABLE OF CONTENTS

1. INTRODUCTION

WELCOME TO WINDOWS 11

Microsoft Windows
Version 23H2 (OS Build 22631.4169)
© Microsoft Corporation. All rights reserved.

The Windows 11 Home operating system and its user interface are protected by trademark and other pending or existing intellectual property rights in the United States and other countries/regions.

Welcome to the exciting world of Windows 11, the latest evolution in Microsoft's long history of groundbreaking operating systems. If you're stepping into Windows 11 for the first time, or considering upgrading from a previous version, this section is designed just for you. We understand that adapting to new technologies can sometimes feel daunting, but don't worry—Windows 11 is built to be both powerful and user-friendly, especially for seniors looking to stay connected and independent.

What is Windows 11?

At its heart, Windows 11 is the new operating system from Microsoft, following Windows 10. It brings several improvements and new features that enhance your computing experience. It's designed to be more secure, more compatible with a variety of devices, and easier to use. It supports activities ranging from the most basic, like writing letters or browsing the internet, to more complex tasks like managing photos or staying safe online.

Why Upgrade to Windows 11?

Windows 11 isn't just a new look; it's a reimagining of what an operating system can do for you. Here's why it might be the right choice:

- **Simplified Design**: The user interface is cleaner and more intuitive, making it easier to find what you need.
- **Improved Performance**: Experience quicker loading times and smoother performance across applications and tasks.
- **Enhanced Security**: With robust built-in protections against viruses and malware, Windows 11 helps protect your personal information and your computer.
- **New Features**: Enjoy new tools and applications designed to help you stay connected with loved ones and maximize your productivity.

Navigating the Basics

Windows 11 is designed with ease of use in mind, especially for those who might feel overwhelmed by new technology.

Here are a few keys to help you feel at home in this new environment:

1. **The Start Menu**: The iconic Start Menu has a new look, positioned in the center of the taskbar, providing easy access to your apps and settings.

2. **Taskbar**: Pin your favorite apps for quick access and view notifications in a clean, organized fashion.

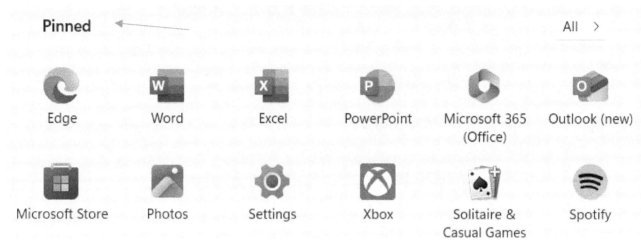

3. **Search function**: Locate documents, apps, or even web content quickly and easily right from the taskbar.
4. **Snap Layouts and Groups**: Easily organize open windows and get back to what you were doing quickly with these new, easy-to-use features.

Every Day Made Easier

For everyday tasks, Windows 11 has you covered with tools and features that simplify your computer use:

- **Widgets**: A new personalized feed powered by AI brings you the news, weather, calendar, and more at a glance.
- **Virtual Desktops**: Set up different desktops for home, work, or play and switch between them with ease.
- **Microsoft Store**: Access a wide range of Microsoft-approved apps that can expand what your computer can do, safely and securely.
- **Microsoft Teams Integration**: Stay in contact with family and friends directly from your desktop with a built-in chat feature.

Staying Safe and Secure

One of the pillars of Windows 11 is its commitment to security. As you explore this new operating system, here are a few elements designed to keep you safe:

- **Windows Defender**: A state-of-the-art antivirus and anti-malware system that is constantly updated to protect against the latest threats.
- **Windows Update**: Automatic updates keep your system secure and functioning optimally without you needing to do a thing.
- **Privacy Settings**: Comprehensive controls allow you to decide what information you share and how your data is used.

Learn at Your Own Pace

Remember, learning a new operating system takes time and practice. Here are a few tips to help you ease into Windows 11:

- **Take Notes**: Keep a notebook handy to jot down new things as you learn them. This can be a great reference as you get more comfortable.
- **Use the Get Started App**: Windows 11 includes a built-in app filled with tutorials and tips to help you navigate the new features.
- **Practice Regularly**: Spending a little bit of time each day using Windows 11 can help you become familiar with its functions more quickly.

Conclusion: Your New Adventure

Think of Windows 11 as a new adventure. With its combination of familiar elements and exciting new features, it offers a fresh, engaging way to interact with your computer. Whether it's staying connected with family, managing your digital photos, or simply enjoying a streamlined, secure computing experience, Windows 11 is here to enhance how you interact with the world. Embrace this journey with curiosity and patience. With each click and swipe, you'll find that Windows 11 is designed to accommodate and facilitate your digital life, making every day a little easier and more connected. Welcome aboard!

WHY WE WROTE THIS BOOK

Technology continues to advance at a breakneck pace, integrating itself more deeply into everyday life. As these developments occur, it's essential that no one gets left behind—especially seniors, who stand to gain enormously from embracing this new digital era. This is where "Windows 11 for Seniors" comes in. **Why did we write this book?** The answer is steeped in passion for accessibility, understanding of technological challenges, and a commitment to empowerment.

Bridging the Digital Gap

At its core, this book emerged from a recognition of the digital gap that often exists for many seniors. As younger generations navigate new technologies almost intuitively, it can seem like older adults are expected to fend for themselves on a playing field that is not always level. Here are specific reasons that motivated the creation of this guide:

1. **Empowerment Through Knowledge**: Knowledge is a powerful tool that fosters independence. By providing you with this knowledge, the book aims to empower you to use Windows 11 confidently, which can open up new channels of communication, information, and entertainment.
2. **Custom-Tailored Content**: Most technology manuals are not written with the senior audience in mind. They often assume a level of familiarity with concepts or jargon that might not be second nature to you. This book addresses this by tailoring content to suit your learning style and familiarity, ensuring it's both accessible and relevant.
3. **Reducing Fear of Technology**: There's often an understandable apprehension about using new technologies because of the fear of making mistakes that can't be undone. This book approaches Windows 11 from a senior's perspective, reducing anxiety by demystifying how things work and providing clear guidance.
4. **Enhancing Everyday Life**: From staying in touch with family and friends via email or video calls to managing appointments and interests online, Windows 11 can significantly enhance daily life. This book helps make those benefits a reality by guiding you through each step with patience and clarity.

Commitment to Clarity and Simplicity

The decision to focus specifically on Windows 11 heralds a commitment to clarity and simplicity:

- **Clear, Jargon-Free Language**: Complex information is broken down into simple, easy-to-understand language. Each feature of Windows 11 is explained without technical jargon, using analogies and examples that relate to everyday experiences.
- **Step-by-Step Instructions**: To ensure you never feel lost, each function and feature of Windows 11 is introduced with step-by-step instructions.
  Whether it's setting up your system or sending an email, the process is laid out clearly with supporting visuals where necessary.
- **Addressing Common Concerns**: Throughout this book, common concerns and questions are addressed proactively. From safeguarding your computer against viruses to ensuring your privacy, each topic is covered thoroughly to build your confidence and competence.

Fostering Connection and Independence

This book aims to not only teach you about an operating system but also to connect you with the broader world through technology. Here's what that looks like:

- **Staying Connected**: Learn how to use tools like Skype, Zoom, or Microsoft Teams effectively to maintain and enhance connections with family and friends.
- **Managing Independence**: From online banking and shopping to accessing health information or simply enjoying hobbies, this guide equips you to handle personal affairs securely and independently.

Encouraging Continuous Learning

"Windows 11 for Seniors" isn't just about the first steps; it's about encouraging an ongoing journey with technology:

- **Building Confidence**: Every chapter is designed to build your confidence, reinforcing skills and encouraging you to explore more features at your own pace.
- **Resources for Continued Learning**: Besides the basics, the book provides resources for further learning, ensuring you have access to support whenever you need it.

Conclusion: Our Vision for Your Digital Journey

The goal of this book is to make sure that technology serves you, not the other way around. By breaking down the barriers to understanding and utilizing Windows 11, we hope to open up a world of possibilities that enhances your independence, safety, and connection to the world. This book is an invitation to a journey—an adventure in the digital world where you are in control. Prepare to harness the power of Windows 11 and transform how you interact with technology every day. Welcome to "Windows 11 for Seniors"—a guidebook for your digital empowerment.

HOW TO USE THIS BOOK EFFECTIVELY

To make the most of "Windows 11 for Seniors," it's crucial to approach this book with a plan and understanding how it's structured to assist you in mastering your new operating system. Whether you're entirely new to the world of computing or upgrading from a previous version of Windows, this guide is tailored to help you navigate the learning process smoothly and efficiently.

Getting Comfortable with the Layout

The layout of this book has been intentionally designed to facilitate easy understanding and practical application. Each chapter builds upon the previous one, ensuring a gradual and comprehensive learning curve. Here's how you can navigate the book:

1. **Sequential Reading**: While it's tempting to jump straight to specific topics, starting from the beginning and proceeding chapter by chapter can be particularly beneficial, as each section prepares you for the next.

2. **Utilize Bookmarks**: Don't hesitate to mark pages you find especially useful. Whether it's a step-by-step tutorial or a particularly insightful tip, having quick access to these sections will aid in reinforcing new skills.

3. **Glossary and Index**: Use the glossary and index to find definitions and key concepts or to quickly locate information on a specific feature or task.

Engaging with the Content

To truly benefit from this book, active engagement with the content is key. Here are some strategies to help you absorb information and turn theory into practice:

- **Hands-On Practice**: As you read each section, have your Windows 11 device in front of you. Follow along with the steps in real-time. The tactile experience of performing the tasks concurrently with the instructions helps solidify your learning.

- **Note-Taking**: Keep a notebook handy for jotting down important points, personal reminders, or questions that you might want to revisit. Writing things down can enhance your memory of new information.

- **Repetition**: Repetition is the mother of skill. Revisit chapters or instructions after your first attempt. You'll likely pick up nuances or details you missed during your first pass.

Translating Instructions to Action

Each tutorial in this book comes with clearly structured instructions, but understanding how to translate these into actions will be crucial:

- **Step-by-Step Follow Through**: Each instruction is laid out in a step-by-step fashion. Make it a point to perform each step one at a time—don't rush. This methodical approach minimizes mistakes and builds your confidence.

- **Use Illustrations**: Wherever there are diagrams, illustrations, or screenshots, spend some time understanding them. Visual aids are great memory boosts and can clarify what text alone might not.

- **Checklists and Tables**: Utilize any checklists or tables provided to track your progress or to understand a process comprehensively. These visual outlines help in breaking down complex tasks into manageable parts.

Challenges and Troubleshooting

Encountering difficulties and challenges is a natural part of the learning process. Here's how you can use this book to troubleshoot common issues:

- **Troubleshooting Guides**: Specific chapters contain troubleshooting tips which address common pitfalls and problems. Refer to these sections if something doesn't work as expected.

- **Asking For Help**: Each chapter concludes with directions or suggestions for further help should you need it. Utilizing these resources can provide answers to more complex questions or problems.

Continuous Learning and Updates

Windows 11, like all technology, is subject to updates and changes. Staying informed about these updates allows you to use Windows 11 more effectively:

- **Update Sections**: Pay special attention to parts of the book dealing with system updates. Knowing how to update your system is critical for maintaining its functionality and security.
- **Online Resources**: Make use of the linkages to online resources where you can find updated information about new features or changes in Windows 11.

Conclusion: Building Confidence Through Mastery

Remember, the goal of using this book is not just to perform tasks, but to understand them deeply enough to feel confident and proficient. With each new chapter and each new task you master, you will find that using your computer becomes more of a pleasure than a challenge. "Windows 11 for Seniors" is your companion on this journey of discovery and mastery—use it well, use it often, and most importantly, use it to unlock all the possibilities that Windows 11 has to offer.

UNDERSTANDING THE BENEFITS OF UPGRADING

Embracing new technology can sometimes feel like a leap into the unknown, but understanding the benefits of upgrading to Windows 11 can help make this transition not just manageable but rewarding. Windows 11 isn't just a new version of a familiar system; it's a significant improvement in ease of use, security, and functionality designed to enhance your computing experience in numerous ways. Let's explore why upgrading to Windows 11 is a beneficial move for seniors.

Enhanced Ease of Use

One of the principal aims of Windows 11 is to provide a more user-friendly experience that caters to users of all ages and tech-savviness, including seniors. Here are some ways in which Windows 11 has improved in terms of usability:

- **Simplified Layout**: The interface is clean and intuitive, with a centered start menu and taskbar that make navigation straightforward. Frequently used apps and settings are easier to find, reducing complexity and improving accessibility.
- **Snap Layouts**: Managing multiple apps and windows is made simpler with Snap Layouts, which allow you to organize your screen with ease. This can be particularly useful when you want to multitask without losing track of open windows.
- **Voice Typing and Commands**: With improved voice recognition technology, carrying out tasks by simply speaking to your computer is more effective than ever, reducing the need to type.

Robust Security and Safety

As technology advances, so too do the threats posed by cyber criminals. Windows 11 has been built with security at its core, offering new and enhanced features to protect your data and your privacy:

- **Improved Windows Defender**: The built-in antivirus software has been upgraded to offer better protection against malware, viruses, and phishing attacks.
- **Hardware-based Integrity Protection**: Windows 11 leverages the latest secure-core PC technologies to protect against firmware and hardware attacks, a level of security previously unavailable in older Windows versions.

- **Privacy Management Tools**: Enhanced privacy settings provide you with clear options to control what data you share and with whom, giving you more control over your digital footprint.

Performance and Efficiency

Speed and responsiveness dramatically affect how enjoyable technology is to use. Windows 11 has been optimized to improve performance, making everyday tasks faster and more responsive:

- **Faster Start Times**: Windows 11 starts up quicker than its predecessors, meaning less waiting time when you turn on your PC.
- **Optimized Resource Allocation**: It uses system resources (like your CPU and RAM) more efficiently, allowing for smoother operation when running multiple applications.
- **DirectStorage**: If you enjoy photography or games, Windows 11 includes new technology like DirectStorage, which loads media much faster than before.

Modern Connectivity and Collaboration

Staying connected with family, friends, and the community is more important than ever. Windows 11 makes this easier with several new technologies designed to support communication:

- **Microsoft Teams Integration**: Teams is now integrated directly into the taskbar, making video calls and meetings just a click away. It's simple to set up and even easier to use for keeping in touch with loved ones.
- **Wi-Fi 6E Support**: With support for the newest Wi-Fi 6E standards, Windows 11 allows for a faster and more stable internet connection, which is vital for smooth video calls and online activities.

Long-Term Support and Sustainability

Upgrading to Windows 11 means benefiting from the latest technology while ensuring your device remains supported and receives important updates:

- **Regular Updates**: Microsoft will provide updates that not only address security issues but also add features and improvements to Windows 11 over time.
- **Energy Efficiency**: Windows 11 is designed to be more energy-efficient, which could help extend the battery life of laptops and reduce energy cost on desktops.

Conclusion: Why Upgrade Matters

Transitioning to Windows 11 is more than just keeping up with technology—it's about making technology work better for you. Whether it's the increased security measures keeping your digital life secure, the performance improvements making your computer faster, or the usability enhancements making daily computing tasks easier and more enjoyable, Windows 11 is designed to enhance your interaction with technology.

The benefits of upgrading extend beyond the physical product, fundamentally elevating your capability to manage personal affairs, enjoy digital hobbies, and stay connected with the world around you. With Windows 11, you're not just keeping pace with technology—you're getting ahead, ensuring a safer, smoother, and more enjoyable computing experience.

2. GETTING STARTED WITH WINDOWS 11

UNBOXING AND SETTING UP YOUR NEW PC

Opening the box of your brand-new PC is always exciting. This chapter will guide you through setting up your new computer, specifically designed with Windows 11. These steps are crafted to ease your journey from unboxing your new device to having it fully operational, tailored just for you.

Step 1: Unboxing Your New PC

Firstly, ensure you have a clean, spacious area to work on. When you're ready, gently remove the PC from its box. Typically, the box will contain:

- The computer itself (laptop or desktop)
- A power cable or adapter
- A user manual
- Possibly a keyboard and a mouse (for desktops)
- Other accessories like a warranty card or a network cable

Tip: It's important to keep all the packaging until you are certain that the computer is working correctly. This packaging will be useful if you need to return or service the unit.

Step 2: Initial Setup

For Desktops: Connect the keyboard and mouse to the computer. These usually plug into the USB ports on the back or front of the computer. Next, connect the monitor by plugging the cable (often VGA, HDMI, or DisplayPort) into the corresponding port on both the monitor and computer. Finally, connect the power cable to the back of the desktop and plug it into an electrical outlet.

For Laptops: Laptops are simpler as they come mostly assembled. Just open the laptop and connect the power adapter. Plug one end into your laptop and the other end into an electrical outlet.

Step 3: Turning On Your Computer

Press the power button. On desktops, it's usually located on the front. Laptops have the power button above the keyboard or on the side. The first time you switch it on, it might take a few minutes longer than usual — this is completely normal.

Step 4: The Out-of-the-Box Experience (OOBE)

Windows 11 guides you through a setup experience known as OOBE, which stands for Out-of-the-Box Experience. Here's what to expect and how to navigate it:

1. **Language and Region:**
   - Select your preferred language and region from the options provided.

2. **Keyboard Layout:**
   - Choose the keyboard layout. You can always add more layouts later in settings if you need them.

3. **Network Connection:**
   - Connect to Wi-Fi by selecting your network from the list and entering the password. If you have an Ethernet cable, connect it to your computer for a wired connection, skipping the Wi-Fi setup.

4. **Microsoft Account:**
   - Sign in with a Microsoft Account. If you don't have one, you can create one during this step. This account helps in synchronizing your settings and files across devices.

5. **Privacy Settings:**
   - You will see options concerning privacy like location tracking, diagnostic data, and targeted ads. Feel free to adjust these according to your comfort and privacy preferences.

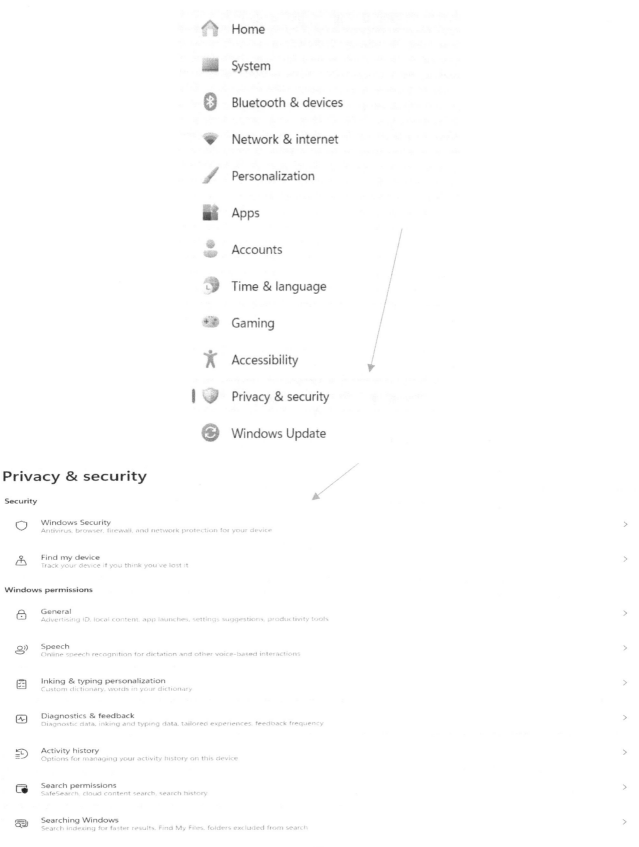

6. **Cortana Setup:**
   o You may be prompted to set up Cortana, Microsoft's virtual assistant. You can enable or skip this step based on your preference.

Step 5: Windows Update

Once setup is complete, Windows 11 may check for updates. It is crucial to install these updates to ensure your computer has the latest security patches and functionality enhancements:

- Follow any on-screen prompts to complete the updates.
- Restart the computer if prompted.

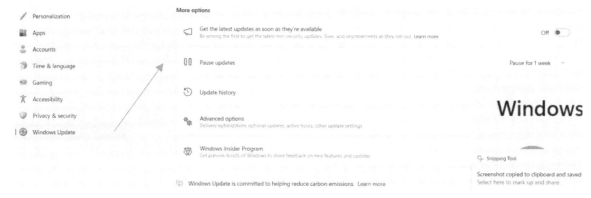

Step 6: Creating Recovery Media

It's wise to create recovery media soon after setup. This is a backup mechanism if your Windows 11 encounters serious issues:

- Search for 'Create recovery drive' in the start menu and follow on-screen instructions.
- You'll need a USB drive with sufficient space as specified by Windows.

Tip: This process can take a long time, so perhaps make a cup of tea while you wait.

Step 7: Explore and Personalize

After these technical steps, take some time to personalize your computer. You can change the desktop background, adjust the display settings, or explore the preinstalled applications. Familiarize yourself with the new features at your own pace, and remember, there is no rush.

Conclusion

Setting up your new PC with Windows 11 should be an enjoyable experience, not a stressful one. Take each step at a time and reach out for help if needed. Remember, this is about making the computer comfortable for you to use, bringing the world of technology into your daily life without hassle.

THE OUT-OF-THE-BOX EXPERIENCE

When you first turn on your new Windows 11 computer, you are greeted with what is known as the Out-of-the-Box Experience (OOBE). This is designed to help you setup essential features and configurations that will make your computer ready for everyday use. Here, we'll walk through each part of this experience to ensure you can customize your setup according to your needs with ease and confidence.

Step-by-Step Guide to the Out-of-the-Box Experience

When your computer starts for the first time, Windows 11 will launch a series of setup screens that guide you through the configuration process. Here's what to expect and how to handle each step:

1. Select Your Language, Time, and Keyboard Preferences

Upon first boot, Windows will ask you to choose your preferred language for the system, the time zone that matches your location, and the keyboard layout you are accustomed to using. These settings can be changed later if needed, but it's best to select them correctly now for your convenience.

- **Language:** Choose the language you are most comfortable with. This will be the language in which all texts, menus, and dialog boxes appear.
- **Time Zone:** Select the correct time zone to ensure your computer's clock is accurate.
- **Keyboard Layout:** Choose the keyboard layout that matches the keyboard you are using. If you're unsure, the standard "US" option is a good starting point for many English-speaking users.

2. Connect to a Network

To get the most out of your Windows 11 experience, you should connect to the internet. This allows you to download the latest updates, sync your settings across devices, and more.

- If you are using Wi-Fi, select your network from the list and enter the password.
- For a wired connection, ensure your Ethernet cable is connected to your computer. Windows should automatically detect this connection.

3. Set Up Your Microsoft Account

A Microsoft Account gives you access to Microsoft services like OneDrive, Office, and Skype. It also allows you to sync your settings and files across devices.

- If you already have a Microsoft Account, enter your email address and password.
- If you do not have an account, you can create one during this step. You'll need to provide some personal information and choose a password.

4. Privacy Settings

Windows 11 will ask you to choose your privacy settings. These control how much data you share with Microsoft and can be adjusted to suit your comfort level.

- You will be presented with options such as location tracking, diagnostic data, tailored experiences, and speech recognition.
- Review each option carefully and toggle each setting on or off based on what you are comfortable with.

5. Customize Your Experience

Windows 11 will ask a few questions to help customize your experience. This might include choosing how you intend to use your computer (for home, school, or work) and what kind of content you're interested in.

- Answer these questions to the best of your ability, as they help Windows tailor the system to your needs.

6. Cortana Setup

Cortana is Windows' built-in digital assistant. During setup, you'll have the option to activate and configure Cortana.

- If you want to use Cortana, follow the prompts to enable the assistant and adjust its settings.
- If you prefer not to use Cortana, you can skip this step.

7. Check for Updates

Once all initial settings have been configured, Windows will check for updates. This is an important process as it ensures your system has all the current security patches and performance improvements.

- Remain connected to the internet and allow your PC to download and install any updates. Restart your computer if prompted.

Final Thoughts

The Out-of-the-Box Experience is structured to ensure that setting up your new computer with Windows 11 is as easy and pain-free as possible. By following these steps, you will have prepared your PC for daily use, customized to your personal preferences and security needs. Remember, take your time and don't feel rushed. It's important that you're comfortable with each decision you make during these initial stages of setting up your new computer.

CREATING AND MANAGING A USER ACCOUNT

One essential step in setting up your new Windows 11 computer is creating and managing your user account. A user account is your personal space within the computer's system, where you can customize your settings, store your files, and manage your applications. Let's walk through how to create your user account and understand the options for managing it effectively.

Creating Your First User Account

During the initial setup of Windows 11, you were asked to sign in with a Microsoft Account or create one. This account becomes your primary user account. Here's more information on what types of accounts you can create and how to manage them:

Types of Accounts

1. **Microsoft Account**: This is an internet-based account that syncs your files, preferences, and settings in the cloud. It allows you to access Microsoft services like OneDrive, Outlook, and Office365 across multiple devices seamlessly.

2. **Local Account**: If you prefer not to use Microsoft's online services, you can choose a local account, which does not require an internet connection to log in to your PC. This account type keeps all your data strictly on the computer.

How to Create a New Account:

1. **Open Settings**: Click the Start button, then select Settings (the gear icon).

Settings

2. **Access Accounts Settings**: In the Settings window, click on "Accounts".

3. **Family & Other Users**: Select "Family & other users" from the side menu.

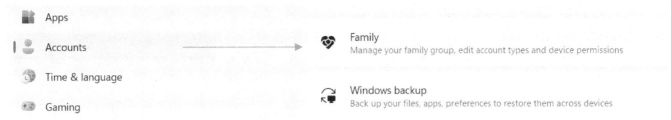

Apps		
Accounts ———————→	♥	**Family** Manage your family group, edit account types and device permissions
Time & language		
Gaming	↻	**Windows backup** Back up your files, apps, preferences to restore them across devices

4. **Add Someone Else to This PC**: Under the "Other users" section, click on "Add someone else to this PC".

Apps	Your family	
Accounts ——————→	Add someone to your family group and allow them to sign in on this device	Add someone
Time & language		

5. **Choose Account Type**:
   - If the person you're adding has a Microsoft account, enter their email address, or for a new account, follow the link to sign them up.
   - To create a local account, select "I don't have this person's sign-in information", then "Add a user without a Microsoft account". Enter a username, password (optional but recommended for security), and password hint.

Managing User Accounts

Once your account is set up, you might need to manage settings or adjust who has access to your PC. Here are some common tasks:

Changing Account Type

- You can change a standard user account to an administrator account or vice versa. Administrators can make system-wide changes, install software, and access all files on the computer.

- **To Change Account Type**:
  1. Go to "Settings > Accounts > Family & other users".
  2. Click on the account you want to change, then select "Change account type".
  3. Choose between Administrator and Standard, then click "OK".

Setting Up Children's Accounts

- Windows 11 allows you to set up specific accounts for children with built-in features to monitor and control their computer activities.

- **To Add a Child's Account**:
  1. Go to "Settings > Accounts > Family & other users".
  2. Under "Your family", click "Add a family member", and select "Add a child".
  3. Follow the prompts to create or log in with their Microsoft account. You can then adjust parental control settings as required.

User Sign-In Options

- Windows 11 offers various sign-in options to access your account, including password, PIN, picture password, facial recognition, and fingerprint, depending on your device's capabilities.

- **To Manage Sign-In Options**:
  1. Go to "Settings > Accounts > Sign-in options".
  2. Choose the sign-in method that best suits your needs and follow the prompts to set it up.

Tips for Managing Your Account and Data

1. **Regularly Update Your Password**: Keeping your password updated is a fundamental step to ensure your data remains secure.

2. **Backup Your Data**: Utilize either OneDrive for cloud backups or an external drive to keep a local backup of essential files.

3. **Review Privacy Settings**: Periodically check and adjust your privacy settings in "Settings > Privacy" to control what data you share with Windows and other users.

Conclusion

Creating and managing your user account on Windows 11 is a foundational step toward a personalized and secure computing experience. By understanding how to set up different types of accounts and manage your sign-in options, you can ensure both ease of access to your personal space on the PC and protection for your personal information. Take these steps seriously, and enjoy a grand experience with your new Windows 11 computer.

UNDERSTANDING WINDOWS 11'S NEW FEATURES

Windows 11 brings a host of new features designed to enhance your computing experience, making it more streamlined, secure, and enjoyable. Whether you're upgrading from a previous version or setting up a new device, these enhancements are set to improve how you interact with your PC on a daily basis. Let's explore these features to better understand how they can simplify and enrich your daily activities.

Simplified Design and User Interface

Start Menu and Taskbar: The Start Menu has been moved to the center of the screen for easier access and consists mainly of pinned apps, recommended files, and a universal search bar. The taskbar is also centered and offers simplified interaction suited for mouse, touch, and pen inputs, making navigation intuitive no matter your preferred method.

Snap Layouts and Snap Groups: These are advanced ways to organize open windows and optimize your screen real estate. By hovering over the maximize button on any open window, you can choose a layout that best suits your current activity, allowing for seamless multitasking.

Enhanced Productivity Tools

Virtual Desktops: Like having multiple monitors on a single screen, Virtual Desktops let you separate different areas of your life—work, personal, hobbies—into individual desktop views. This can be managed from the taskbar, allowing easy switching between each desktop environment.

Microsoft Teams Integration: A chat feature from Microsoft Teams is integrated directly into the taskbar, making it easier to connect with contacts through text, chat, video, or voice. This feature ensures that staying in touch with family, friends, and colleagues is just a click away.

Improved Performance and Efficiency

Faster Wake from Sleep: Windows 11 has been optimized to wake from sleep almost instantly, ensuring that you can continue right where you left off without waiting.

Windows Hello for Faster Sign-in: This security feature uses face recognition or fingerprint scanning to quickly log you in. This method is not only faster but also more secure than typing a password.

Updated Microsoft Store and Android Apps

Revamped Microsoft Store: The new Microsoft Store is easier to navigate and offers a larger variety of apps than ever before, now including Android apps through Amazon's Appstore. This integration means you can now use your favorite mobile apps right on your desktop.

Accessibility Improvements

Voice Typing and Voice Commands: Windows 11 includes improved voice typing with auto-punctuation and voice commands, making it easier to interact with your computer hands-free. This is especially useful for drafting emails or navigating without relying on a keyboard.

Accessibility Settings: Enhanced settings include new themes, magnifier improvements, and better read-aloud options, all designed to make Windows more accessible to users with various levels of ability.

Security Enhancements

Hardware-based Security: Windows 11 requires devices to have hardware-based security features turned on, such as TPM 2.0 (Trusted Platform Module), which helps protect against malware and ransomware.

Microsoft Defender SmartScreen: This automatically helps protect you from malicious websites and downloads, ensuring that your online experience is safe and secure.

Widgets

Widgets are a new addition to Windows 11, offering at-a-glance information like news, weather, calendar, and to-do lists. They are accessible from the taskbar and can be personalized according to your interests and needs.

Eco-Friendly Features

In line with global sustainability efforts, Windows 11 includes features aimed at reducing carbon footprint. This includes optimized battery usage for laptops and scheduled updates to occur during times of lower carbon emissions based on regional electricity data.

Why These Features Matter

Understanding and utilizing these new features helps ensure you're making the most of your Windows 11 experience. The design's emphasis on simplicity and efficiency can transform how you interact with your PC, making it not only more intuitive but also more enjoyable. From enhanced security measures to accessibility improvements, Windows 11 is crafted to provide a robust, user-friendly platform suited for today's digital age.

By mastering these features, you'll be able to navigate your computer with greater confidence and ease, ensuring that technology remains a helpful, rather than daunting, part of your everyday life.

3. THE WINDOWS 11 INTERFACE

NAVIGATING THE START MENU

Navigating the Start Menu on your Windows 11 computer is like discovering the gateway to all the wonderful tools and features your computer has to offer. Think of it as a personal concierge desk: one click, and you have a menu at your service, guiding you towards the applications, settings, and documents you need. Let's explore how to use this efficiently, so you can enjoy a smooth and friendly user experience.

Understanding the Start Menu Layout

When you click the Start button (which looks like a Windows logo) at the bottom left corner of your screen, a panel pops up. This panel is divided into three main sections:

1. **Pinned Apps**: Here, you'll see icons for applications you use frequently. You can customize this section by adding or removing app icons according to your needs.

2. **All Apps**: By clicking on 'All Apps' you can view a list of all the software applications installed on your computer.

3. **Recommended**: This section automatically displays recently opened files and frequently used apps to provide quick access.

How to Customize Your Pinned Apps

Customizing your Pinned Apps makes accessing your favorite and most-used applications easier:

1. **To Pin an App**:
   o Click on the Start button.

   o Scroll to find the app in the 'All Apps' list or type its name in the search bar at the top.

Pinned   All >

   o Right-click on the app and choose 'Pin to Start'.

      o   The app icon will now appear in the Pinned Apps area.

  2. **To Unpin an App**:

      o   Right-click on the app icon you want to remove from the Pinned Apps area.

      o   Select 'Unpin from Start'.

      o   The icon will be removed, but the app will remain on your computer.

Searching for Apps and Files

If you can't see the application or file you need immediately, Windows 11's Start Menu has a powerful search feature:

1. Click the Start button.
2. Start typing the name of the application, document, or setting you're looking for.
3. Results will appear as you type, categorically divided - apps, documents, web results, and more.

Using this search bar significantly reduces the time you spend looking for things, acting like a quick assistant ready at your command.

Using The "Recommended" Section

The Recommended section offers a quick snapshot of your recent activities on the computer. It's like having a small diary that keeps note of what you've used recently so you can quickly jump back in:

1. To open a file, just click on it in the Recommended section.
2. If you want to see more items, there is often an option to expand this list by selecting 'More' at the bottom of the section.

This area is dynamic, updating throughout the day as you open and work on different things.

Adjust Settings Directly from the Start Menu

For quicker access to your system settings:

1. Click on the Start button.
2. Select the settings gear icon, typically found pinned on the Start Menu.
3. This opens the Settings app where you can adjust various aspects of your computer like System, Devices, Phone, Network & Internet, Personalization, and more.

Logging Off or Switching Users

The Start Menu also allows you to switch users or log off from your account:

1. Click the Start button.
2. Select your user icon at the bottom of the Start Menu.
3. Choose 'Sign out' or 'Switch user' based on your needs.

This feature is useful when multiple people use the same device or when you need to securely log out.

Restart or Shut Down Your Computer

Finally, when you've finished using your computer, you can turn it off or restart it:

1. Click the Start button.
2. Select the power icon found at the bottom of the Start Menu.
3. Choose 'Shut down' or 'Restart'.

Remember, shutting down your computer when not in use can help save energy and extend your PC's life.

Summing Up

By mastering the Start Menu, you've essentially learned how to quickly navigate to any application, setting, or document on your Windows 11 PC. Customizing your Start Menu by pinning frequently used apps and taking advantage of the search functionality can make your daily computer use much more efficient. This foundational skill ensures you can confidently explore more complex features at your leisure. Remember, practice makes perfect, and the more you use these features, the more intuitive they will become!

TASKBAR AND SYSTEM TRAY ESSENTIALS

The Taskbar and System Tray on your Windows 11 computer serve as a control panel for easy access to apps, notifications, and system functions that you use frequently. Understanding how to effectively use these tools will enhance your computing experience, making it more organized and less overwhelming.

Exploring the Taskbar

The Taskbar is the horizontal bar at the bottom of your screen, traditionally aligned in the center in Windows 11, and it includes several functionalities:

1. **Start Button**: Clicking this opens the Start Menu, which is your gateway to applications, settings, and files.

2. **Search Icon**: This allows you to search directly in your computer for files, apps, or even results from the web.

3. **Task View**: This icon lets you view all open windows at once or access multiple desktops for better organization of your tasks.

4. **Widgets**: Clicking here displays a pane with news, weather, and other info - think of it as your personal digital newspaper.

5. **Chat**: Quick access to Microsoft Teams enables you to chat or video call friends and family.

Microsoft Teams

App

Using the Taskbar for Quick App Access

You can pin your most used applications to the Taskbar for quick access:

1. **To Pin an App**:
   - Find the app in the Start Menu.
   - Right-click the app and select 'More' followed by 'Pin to Taskbar'.
   - The app's icon will now sit on the Taskbar for speedy access.

2. **To Unpin an App**:
   - Right-click the app icon on the Taskbar.
   - Select 'Unpin from taskbar'.
   - The icon will disappear from the Taskbar but will remain available on your system.

These simple steps can make your favorite tools just a click away, streamlining your day-to-day tasks.

Managing Open Windows via the Taskbar

The Taskbar shows icons for all applications currently running on your computer:

1. Clicking an icon on the Taskbar will bring that application's window to the forefront.
2. If an application has multiple windows open, a small icon overlay or a stacked effect on the Taskbar icon indicates this. Clicking the icon will display thumbnails of all open windows.

Using these visuals, you can quickly switch between tasks without cluttering your screen.

The System Tray: A Hub for Quick Settings and Notifications

On the right end of the Taskbar lies the System Tray, also known as the notification area. It contains several functional icons:

1. **Network Icon**: Click to connect to a Wi-Fi network or troubleshoot internet issues.

2. **Volume Icon**: Adjust the sound level or mute audio.

3. **Battery Icon**: Laptop users can check the battery status or change power settings.

4. **Notification Center**: Displays new emails, app notifications, and reminders.

Clicking on these icons allows you to make quick changes without navigating through multiple settings pages.

Customizing the Taskbar

Ensuring your Taskbar suits your needs is key for an enjoyable computer experience:

1. **To Move the Taskbar**:
   - Right-click an empty area on the Taskbar.
   - Select 'Taskbar settings'.
   - Under 'Taskbar behaviors', you can change the alignment or automatically hide the Taskbar.

2. **Change Taskbar Color:**

   o In 'Taskbar settings', go to 'Personalization'.

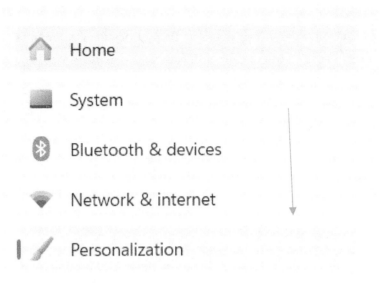

   o Choose 'Colors' and pick a color that you like for the Taskbar.

Recent colors

Windows colors

3. **To Rearrange Icons on the Taskbar:**
    o Click and drag an icon to a new position on the Taskbar.
    o This lets you organize your frequently used apps according to your preference.

Notification Center and Calendar

Clicking on the date and time in your System Tray opens up the Notification Center and Calendar:

1. **Notification Center**: Keeps all your recent notifications in one place. You can clear them all at once or one by one.
2. **Calendar**: Provides a quick glance at your schedule. You can also add appointments or reminders directly from this view.

Calendar
App

This integration helps keep your day organized without needing to open a separate app.

Restarting or Shutting Down from the Taskbar

If you need to restart or shut down your computer:

1. Right-click the Start button.
2. Select 'Shut down or sign out'.
3. Choose from the options to shut down, restart, or put your computer to sleep.

Concluding Thoughts

Understanding and customizing the Taskbar and System Tray in Windows 11 can significantly simplify your digital environment. By arranging these spaces to your comfort, you can access essential applications, adjust key settings, and stay updated with notifications—all from a single bar. As you become more familiar with these tools, your interactions with your PC will become more intuitive and efficient, making every session enjoyable and productive. Remember, exploring these features at your own pace is perfectly fine. With each step, you're mastering more of your computer's capabilities.

USING VIRTUAL DESKTOPS

Imagine having multiple desks in your workspace, each dedicated to a different project or type of activity. Virtual desktops in Windows 11 are somewhat akin to this concept. They allow you to organize your computer applications and windows into separate, easily manageable groups. This can be especially helpful if you like to keep tasks like email, browsing, and photo editing distinct and tidy. Here's how to harness the power of virtual desktops to increase your efficiency and enjoy a clutter-free digital environment.

What Are Virtual Desktops? - Virtual desktops are separate workspaces on your computer. Each desktop displays only the applications and windows pertaining to a particular task or use. For example, you might have one desktop for general web browsing, another for managing photos and videos, and yet another for writing or number crunching. This keeps your screen from becoming overcrowded and helps focus on one group of tasks at a time.

How to Access and Use Virtual Desktops

Accessing and managing your virtual desktops in Windows 11 is straightforward. Here's a step-by-step guide to get you started:

1. **Opening Virtual Desktops**:
   - Click on the Task View icon on the Taskbar (it looks like two overlapping rectangles), or simply press Win + Tab on your keyboard. Here, you'll see all open windows and any virtual desktops you have set up at the bottom of the screen.

2. **Creating a New Virtual Desktop**:
   - In the Task View pane, click on the New desktop button, which appears at the top left corner. Each click will create a new virtual desktop.
   - Alternatively, you can press Win + Ctrl + D to create a new desktop without opening the Task View.

3. **Switching Between Desktops**:
   - Open the Task View pane.
   - Click on the desktop you want to view. You can also switch between desktops using the keyboard shortcuts Win + Ctrl + Left Arrow or Win + Ctrl + Right Arrow for back and forth movement.

4. **Moving Windows Between Desktops**:
   - Open the Task View.
   - Drag a window from its current desktop to the desired one. Alternatively, right-click on the window in the Task View and select 'Move to' and then choose the desktop you'd like to move it to.

5. **Closing Virtual Desktops**:
   - Open the Task View.
   - Hover over the desktop you want to close and click the small 'x' that appears in the upper right corner of the desktop preview.
   - Any open applications on that desktop will automatically move to your next active desktop.

Tips for Organizing Virtual Desktops

To make the most out of virtual desktops, consider how you might organize your activities:

- **Desktop for Daily Tasks**: Email communication, calendar events, and other everyday apps.
- **Reading and Research Desktop**: Browser windows for reading online articles, eBooks, or researching.
- **Hobby or Leisure Desktop**: Streaming services, social media, or hobby-related applications.

This division not only helps keep related tasks together but also minimizes distraction when focusing on a specific job.

Advantages of Using Virtual Desktops

- **Increased Focus**: Less clutter means fewer distractions, helping you focus on the task at hand.
- **Easier Navigation**: With dedicated desktops, you know exactly where to find the applications and documents you are working with.
- **Flexibility**: Easily switch between tasks without losing your place in open applications or documents.

Customizing and Personalizing Virtual Desktops

Although Windows 11 doesn't allow different backgrounds for each desktop, you can still adopt certain strategies to personalize your experience:

- **Name Your Desktops**: Right-click on the desktop thumbnail in Task View and select 'Rename'. Giving each desktop a specific name like 'Finance', 'Family', or 'Projects' can further enhance your organization strategy.

Mastering Virtual Desktops

Remember, the key to effectively using virtual desktops is consistency. Keep your desktop arrangements logical and consistent, so you automatically know which desktop to switch to for a given task. Practice navigating, creating, and managing these desktops to become more comfortable with their use. By integrating virtual desktops into your daily computer use, you effectively create a tidy workspace that mirrors a well-organized physical office. This can make your computing experience not only more enjoyable but also significantly more efficient. With these simple steps, you're well on your way to mastering a feature that can transform how you interact with your Windows 11 PC, making your digital life as orderly as your real one.

CUSTOMIZING YOUR START MENU

Customizing the Start Menu on your Windows 11 computer allows you to tailor this central hub to your specific needs, enabling quicker access to your most-used applications, files, and settings. With a few simple tweaks, you can make the Start Menu a powerful, personalized tool that enhances your computing experience.

Understand the Default Start Menu Layout

Before you begin customizing, it's important to familiarize yourself with the basic elements of the Start Menu:

- **Pinned Apps Section**: This is where your frequently used apps can be pinned for quick access.
- **All Apps Button**: A list that shows every application installed on your computer.
- **Recommended Section**: Displays recently opened files and frequently used apps.
- **User Account**: Your profile picture and related options, including account settings and the ability to lock or sign out.
- **Power Button**: For shutting down, restarting, or putting the computer to sleep.

Customizing Pinned Apps

You can easily customize which applications are pinned to the Start Menu for rapid access:

1. **Pin an App**:
   - Open 'All Apps'.
   - Right-click on the app you wish to pin.
   - Select 'Pin to Start'.
   - The app will now appear in the 'Pinned Apps' section.

2. **Unpin an App**:
   - Right-click on the app icon in the 'Pinned Apps' section.
   - Select 'Unpin from Start'.
   - The app icon will be removed but will remain installed on your system.

3. **Reorder Pinned Apps**:
   - Click and drag the app icons in the 'Pinned Apps' section to rearrange them according to your preference.

Customizing the Layout

Windows 11 allows you to adjust how these elements are displayed:

1. **Resize the Start Menu**:
   o Hover your mouse at the edge of the Start Menu until you see the resize cursor.
   o Click and drag to adjust the size vertically or horizontally.

2. **Choose More Pins or More Recommendations**:
   o Right-click any empty space in the Start Menu and go to 'Settings'.
   o In the 'Start Menu' settings, you can choose to show more pinned items or more recommendations by adjusting the layout options.

Using Folders in the Start Menu

Organizing apps into folders can help keep your Start Menu tidy and more manageable:

1. **Create a Folder**:
   o Drag one app icon over another in the 'Pinned Apps' section. This will automatically create a folder.
   o You can name the folder by opening it and clicking on the folder name area at the top.

2. **Adding Apps to Folders**:
   o Drag and drop other apps into the folder.

3. **Remove Apps from Folders**:
   o Open the folder and drag the app out of it back to the 'Pinned Apps' area.

Personalizing with Live Tiles - Some applications support Live Tiles, which display dynamically updated content such as new emails or weather updates:

1. **Enable/Disable Live Tiles**:
   o Right-click on an app that supports Live Tiles.
   o Toggle the 'Turn Live Tile on/off' option.

Adjusting Start Menu Settings

For further personalization, you can adjust various settings related to the Start Menu:

1. **Show App List in Start Menu**:
   o Go to Settings > Personalization > Start.
   o Toggle 'Show app list in Start menu' to choose whether the list of all apps is displayed by default.

2. **Show Recently Added Apps and Most Used Apps**:
   o In the same 'Start' settings, adjust the toggles for showing recently added apps and most used apps according to your preference.

3. **Choose Which Folders Appear on Start**:
   o Still in the 'Start' settings, you can select 'Folders' and choose which shortcuts like Settings, Documents, or Downloads appear directly on the Start Menu.

Consistency and Usability - Maintaining a consistent and deliberate layout in your Start Menu can help reduce confusion and enhance usability. Organize it in a way that feels natural to you, prioritizing easy access to the apps and files you use most. By learning to customize the Start Menu to suit your habits and preferences, you effectively minimize the time spent searching for apps or settings and maximize your efficiency. It's about setting up your digital workspace just the way you like it, making every day interactions with your Windows 11 computer easier and more enjoyable. With these skills, you'll feel more in control of your computer environment, promoting a more fulfilling and efficient digital experience.

4. BASIC OPERATIONS

OPENING AND CLOSING PROGRAMS

Welcome to the world of Windows 11, where understanding the basics can open up an array of opportunities. One fundamental skill you'll find invaluable is knowing how to open and close programs on your computer. This might sound simple, but it's the cornerstone of efficient computer usage. Let's take this step-by-step, ensuring you grasp each part without feeling overwhelmed.

How to Open Programs

Opening a program in Windows 11 can be done in various ways. We'll explore some of the most user-friendly methods. Remember, practice makes perfect, so don't hesitate to try these steps as you read through.

Using the Start Menu

The Start Menu is your gateway to all the applications installed on your PC.

1. **Click the Start button**: This is found at the bottom-left corner of your screen and looks like the Windows logo.
2. **Browse or search for an application**: Once you click the Start button, you can either scroll through a list of applications or use the search bar at the top of the Start Menu to type the name of the program you're looking for.
3. **Click on the application name**: Once you find it, simply click on it, and the program will open.

For instance, if you want to open Microsoft Word, you would click the Start button, type "Word" in the search bar, and then click on the Word icon when it appears.

Using Desktop Shortcuts

Desktop shortcuts allow you to open programs right from your desktop, without navigating menus.

1. **Identify the program's shortcut icon**: These are small images that represent the program you want to open, usually found on your desktop.
2. **Double-click on the shortcut icon**: By double-clicking (clicking your mouse button twice rapidly), the program will start up.

Using the Taskbar

The taskbar is located at the bottom of your screen and can hold icons for frequently-used programs.

1. **Find the program icon on your taskbar**: If you've pinned your frequently used programs here, their icons will be visible.
2. **Click on the icon**: A single click is enough to open the program.

This method is particularly useful for programs you use frequently, like your web browser or email client.

How to Close Programs

Now that you've opened a program, let's learn how to close it properly. This is important to keep your computer running smoothly.

Using the 'X' Button

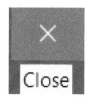

Every Windows program will have an 'X' button at the top right corner of its window – this is the universal symbol for closing applications.

1. **Locate the 'X' button**: Look at the top right of the program's window.
2. **Click the 'X' button**: This will close the program.

Using Alt + F4 Shortcut

Keyboard shortcuts can be very efficient. Alt + F4 is a powerful shortcut that closes the current active program.

1. **Make sure the program you want to close is active**: Click anywhere within the program window or click its icon on the taskbar to make sure it's selected.
2. **Press Alt + F4 together**: This will close the program immediately.

Using Task Manager

If a program isn't responding and you can't close it the normal way, the Task Manager is a useful tool.

1. **Open Task Manager**: Press Ctrl + Shift + Esc on your keyboard.
2. **Find the program in the list**: There will be a list of all running applications.
3. **Click on the program and select 'End Task'**: This will force the program to close.

This method should be used sparingly, as it can cause you to lose unsaved work.

Practice Makes Perfect

Don't be discouraged if these steps seem awkward at first. With a little practice, they will become second nature. Remember, each time you open or close a program, you are building your confidence and mastering your new Windows 11 computer.

Conclusion

Opening and closing programs are essential skills that form the basis of interacting with your PC. Start with these simple methods, and as you grow more comfortable, you'll find navigating Windows 11 an enjoyable and empowering experience. Remember, each interaction is a step toward becoming adept with your computer, so keep practicing and exploring.

BASIC TYPING AND TEXT EDITING

Typing and editing text on a computer is a crucial skill that can enhance your daily computer use, especially when crafting emails, organizing documents, or even jotting down some notes. In Windows 11, basic typing and text editing are straightforward processes that can be mastered with a little practice. Let's walk through the essentials, using user-friendly steps to ensure you're comfortable and confident in your abilities.

Getting Started with Typing

Before diving into more complex editing techniques, it's important to feel at ease with typing.

Opening a Text Editor

One simple tool you can use for typing is Notepad, a basic text editor included with Windows 11.

1. **Open Notepad**: Click on the Start Menu, type "Notepad," and select it from the results. This will open a blank document.

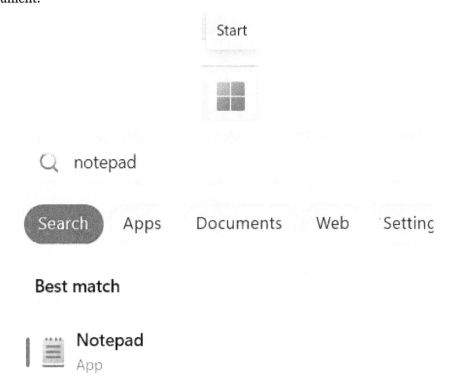

2. **Start typing**: Click anywhere on the blank document and begin typing. The blinking vertical line you see is called the cursor, and it indicates where your next character will appear.

As you type, you might make mistakes. Don't worry! Mistakes are part of learning. If you misspell a word or want to change what you wrote, simply use the Backspace key (located above the Enter key) to delete characters one by one.

Selecting Text

To edit or format parts of your text, you first need to know how to select it.

1. **Click and Drag**: Place your cursor at the beginning of the text you want to select, click the left mouse button, hold it down, and drag your mouse over the text.
2. **Shift and Arrow Keys**: Click at the start of the text, hold down the Shift key, and use the arrow keys to extend the selection in the direction you want.

Cut, Copy, and Paste

These are fundamental skills that allow you to move or replicate your text efficiently.

Cutting Text

Cutting text removes it from the original location and stores it on the clipboard (a temporary storage area in Windows).

1. **Select the text** you want to cut.
2. **Right-click the selection** and choose "Cut", or press Ctrl+X on your keyboard.

Copying Text

Copying text copies the selected text to the clipboard without removing it from the original location.

1. **Select the text** you want to copy.
2. **Right-click the selection** and choose "Copy", or press Ctrl+C.

Pasting Text

Pasting places the last text cut or copied into the clipboard to where you place your cursor.

1. **Click** where you want the text to go.
2. **Right-click** and choose "Paste", or press Ctrl+V.

Basic Text Formatting

Even though Notepad is quite basic, other programs like Microsoft Word provide more formatting options. Here's how you can change the appearance of your text in a more advanced text editor:

1. **Bold**: To make your text bold, select the text, then click the "B" icon or press Ctrl+B.
2. **Italics**: To italicize your text, select it, then click the "I" icon or press Ctrl+I.
3. **Underline**: To underline your text, select it, then click the "U" icon or press Ctrl+U.

Undo and Redo

If you make a mistake or change your mind about an edit:

1. **Undo**: Press Ctrl+Z. This will undo your last action.
2. **Redo**: If you undid something by mistake, press Ctrl+Y to redo it.

Using Spell Check

In programs like Microsoft Word, spell check is a helpful tool to correct spelling errors:

1. **Right-click on a word** underlined in red (indicating a spelling error).
2. **Choose the correct spelling** from the list of suggestions.

Saving Your Document

To avoid losing your work, save your document frequently:

1. **Click File** in the top left corner.
2. **Choose Save As**.
3. **Select where to save your file**, type a filename, and click "Save".

Practice Regularly

The more you practice typing and editing text, the more comfortable you will become. Don't rush through the steps; instead, take your time to understand and memorize them.

To enhance your new skills, engage in daily typing exercises or compose a short journal entry or email to a friend. Every bit of practice will help solidify your confidence and proficiency.

Through understanding these basics of typing and text editing within Windows 11, you're well on your way to becoming more adept at navigating and utilizing your computer, thereby enhancing your overall experience and ability to communicate effectively in the digital age.

USING THE CLIPBOARD: CUT, COPY, AND PASTE

Mastering the use of the clipboard to cut, copy, and paste text is similar to learning how to use essential tools in a toolbox. It's about moving or duplicating things, not with physical objects, but with words and images on your computer. This functionality is vital for managing documents and emails efficiently or organizing information on your Windows 11 system. Let's navigate through this process with clear, easy steps to make you comfortable using these essential features.

Understanding the Clipboard

The clipboard is a special storage area in your computer's memory that temporarily holds information when you cut or copy something. When you paste, Windows 11 transfers that information from the clipboard to the place where you want it to go. Think of it as a temporary shelf where your copied content sits until you decide where to put it permanently.

How to Cut, Copy, and Paste Text

These three actions are foundational to managing your digital content. Whether you're organizing files, editing documents, or sending emails, these skills will prove invaluable.

1. Cutting Text

Cutting text removes it from its original location and places it into the clipboard. It's useful when you want to move text from one place to another.

- **Select the text**: Click and drag your mouse over the text you want to move.
- **Cut the text**:
  - **Using the mouse**: Right-click on the highlighted text and select "Cut."
  - **Using the keyboard**: Press Ctrl+X.

2. Copying Text

Copying text duplicates it from the original source to the clipboard, leaving the original text unchanged. It is perfect when you need to duplicate text within a document or into another document.

- **Select the text**: Similar to cutting, click and drag your mouse over the text you want to copy.
- **Copy the text**:
  - **Using the mouse**: Right-click on the highlighted text and choose "Copy."
  - **Using the keyboard**: Press Ctrl+C.

3. Pasting Text

Pasting is how you move or copy the clipboard's content to a new location in the same or a different document.

- **Place your cursor**: Click where you want the cut or copied text to go.
- **Paste the text**:
  - **Using the mouse**: Right-click and choose "Paste."
  - **Using the keyboard**: Press Ctrl+V.

Practical Uses of Cut, Copy, and Paste

Here are a few practical examples to help you understand when and how to use these commands:

- **Organizing Documents**: When organizing files or folders, you may want to move items from one folder to another. Cutting and pasting can simplify this task.
- **Editing an Email**: If you're composing an email and want to rearrange the paragraphs, you can cut and paste the paragraphs into their new positions.
- **Creating a Reference Document**: If you're doing research and gathering information from various sources, you can copy information from web pages or PDFs and paste it into a Word document.

Tips for Effective Use

- **Use Keyboard Shortcuts**: Learning the keyboard shortcuts for cut, copy, and paste (Ctrl+X, Ctrl+C, and Ctrl+V respectively) can speed up your work significantly.
- **Be Mindful When Cutting**: Since cutting removes the text from its original location, be sure you want to move the text before you cut it.
- **Check Your Clipboard**: Since the clipboard holds only the last cut or copied item, ensure you paste your copied content before you cut or copy again to avoid losing data.

Troubleshooting Common Issues

Sometimes, you might run into problems with cutting, copying, and pasting. Here's how to handle a few common issues:

- **Text Not Pasting Correctly**: Make sure you've actually copied or cut something before you try to paste it. If you're switching between applications, wait a few seconds for the software to catch up.
- **Text Format Changes After Pasting**: If the formatting changes unexpectedly when you paste, try using "Paste Special" or "Keep Text Only" options in applications like Microsoft Word.

Conclusion

The abilities to cut, copy, and paste are more than just functions - they are essential tools that, once mastered, will enhance your navigation and operation within Windows 11, making your computer use more efficient and less time-consuming. By practicing these fundamental skills, you'll find that handling documents, emails, and other digital content is a breeze. So, give these tasks a try, and soon you'll move and duplicate text as smoothly as turning the pages of your favorite book.

<h2 style="text-align:center">SWITCHING BETWEEN APPLICATIONS</h2>

As you begin to feel more at ease using your Windows 11 computer, you'll find that multitasking—doing several activities at once—becomes a necessity. This might involve switching from writing an email to browsing the internet or checking your photos while editing a document. Learning how to switch between different applications efficiently can enhance your computing experience, letting you manage multiple tasks without stress. Here's how you can master this skill with simple, easy-to-follow steps.

Understanding Task View and Alt+Tab

Windows 11 provides several ways to switch between your open applications. Two of the most user-friendly and common techniques are using the Task View and the Alt+Tab keyboard shortcut.

Using Task View

Task View is a feature in Windows 11 that displays all your open windows at once, making it easy to switch between them.

1. **Open Task View**:
   - Click the Task View icon on the taskbar. It looks like two overlapping rectangles next to the Start icon.
   - Alternatively, you can press Win + Tab on your keyboard.
2. **Switch between applications**:
   - Once open, Task View will show thumbnails of all your open applications.
   - Click on the window you wish to bring to the forefront of your screen.

Task View also allows you to create virtual desktops, which can be helpful if you want to organize your tasks by desktop, keeping leisure activities separate from work-related tasks.

Using Alt+Tab

The Alt+Tab shortcut is perhaps the quickest way to switch between running applications.

1. **Press and hold the Alt key on your keyboard, then tap the Tab key.**
   - You'll see small icons representing each open application appear in a row on your screen.
2. **Continue holding the Alt key and press the Tab key repeatedly** to cycle through the icons.
3. **Release the Alt key** when the desired application's icon is highlighted to switch to that application.

This method is highly effective when working with several programs and needing to switch quickly.

Switching Using the Taskbar

Your taskbar, located at the bottom of your screen, is another tool for switching applications.

1. **Identify the application icon**:
   - Look at the taskbar; you will see icons for applications you have pinned there or that are currently running.
2. **Click the application icon**:
   - Simply clicking on an app's icon will bring it to the forefront.
   - If the application is minimized, clicking the icon will maximize it onto your screen.

If you have multiple windows of the same application open, hovering your cursor over the icon will show a preview of all the open windows. Click on the preview of the window you want to switch to.

Closing Unneeded Applications

It's a good habit to close applications that you are not using to free up resources on your PC.

1. **Switch to the application you want to close** using any of the methods mentioned above.
2. **Close the application**:
   - Click the 'X' at the top right of the window.
   - Alternatively, right-click the application's icon on the taskbar and choose 'Close window'.

Maintaining only necessary applications open can help your computer run more smoothly and allow you to focus on the task at hand.

Troubleshooting

Sometimes, applications may not switch correctly, or you might find that your computer is not responding when you try to switch.

- **If an application is not responding**: You can right-click the application in taskbar and select 'Close window'. If that fails, using Task Manager to end the application might be necessary.
- **If shortcuts don't work**: Ensure your keyboard is functioning correctly. Sometimes, external keyboards may have settings that need adjustments or require specific drivers.

Practice Makes Perfect

Switching between applications might seem trivial, but it's a core skill in mastering efficient computer use. As you continue to practice these maneuvers, they will become second nature. Start by opening a few different applications like a web browser, Word processor, and perhaps a photo viewer. Practice using Task View, Alt+Tab, and switching via the taskbar until the process feels smooth and effortless.

The ability to juggle various applications efficiently using these methods will not only save you time but also enhance your overall experience as you navigate through your daily tasks on your computer. Remember, the key to mastery is consistent practice and patience.

5. CONNECTING TO THE INTERNET

SETTING UP WI-FI AND ETHERNET CONNECTIONS

Windows 11 brings a myriad of opportunities to connect to the world, and setting up your internet connection is the first step towards exploring the vast digital universe. Whether you are reaching out to family, shopping online, or exploring new hobbies, a stable internet connection is your gateway to these activities. This section will guide you through setting up both Wi-Fi and Ethernet connections on your new Windows 11 computer in a simple, straightforward manner.

Understanding Your Internet Connection Options

There are two primary ways to connect your computer to the internet:

1. **Wi-Fi (Wireless):** Wi-Fi allows you to connect to the internet wirelessly. It's convenient if you prefer to use your computer in different locations around your home without a physical cable.

2. **Ethernet (Wired):** An Ethernet connection uses a cable to connect your computer to the internet. It is typically faster and more stable than a Wi-Fi connection, which makes it ideal for activities that require a lot of data like watching videos or downloading large files.

Setting Up a Wi-Fi Connection

Step 1: Locate the Network Icon

- On the bottom right corner of your taskbar, you will find the network icon. It looks like a small globe or Wi-Fi symbol. Click on this icon.

Step 2: Connect to a Network

- A list of available wireless networks will appear. These are the Wi-Fi networks in range of your computer.
- Find the name of your Wi-Fi network (often referred to as the SSID), which you might have set up yourself or was set by your Internet Service Provider. If you're unsure, it can usually be found on your Wi-Fi router.

Step 3: Enter the Wi-Fi Password

- Click on your Wi-Fi network, and you will be prompted to enter a password. This password is also usually provided by your ISP and often found on your router.
- Type the password carefully. Remember that passwords are case-sensitive. If you make a mistake, don't worry; just clear it and type it again.

Step 4: Connect and Test Your Connection

- After entering the password, click "Connect."
- Once connected, the network icon will change to indicate a successful connection. You can test this by opening a web browser and trying to visit a website like www.google.com.

Setting Up an Ethernet Connection

Step 1: Locate Your Ethernet Port

- Find the Ethernet port on your computer. It looks a bit like a standard telephone jack, but slightly larger.
- If your computer does not have an Ethernet port, you might need an adapter.

Step 2: Connect the Ethernet Cable

- Take one end of the Ethernet cable and plug it into the port on your computer. Make sure it clicks into place.
- Connect the other end to one of the out ports on your router or modem.

Step 3: Confirm Connection

- There's no need to enter a password as you might with Wi-Fi.

- Your computer should automatically detect the internet connection. You will see the network icon on the system tray change to indicate a successful Ethernet connection.
- Test the connection by opening your browser and visiting a website.

Tips for Enhancing Your Internet Experience

- **Positioning Your Router:** For Wi-Fi users, try to position your router in a central location in your home away from walls and metal objects to maximize signal strength.
- **Regular Updates:** Keep your Wi-Fi router's software up to date to ensure your network is secure and performing well.
- **Manage Wi-Fi Networks:** If your Wi-Fi list becomes cluttered, you can manage networks by forgetting ones you no longer use. Simply click on the network icon, right-click on the network you want to forget, and select "Forget."

Troubleshooting Common Issues

- **No Internet Connection:** Check to ensure that both ends of your Ethernet cable are securely connected. For Wi-Fi, ensure that your router is turned on and the password typed is correct.
- **Slow Internet Speed:** Restart your router by unplugging it, waiting for about 60 seconds, and plugging it back in. Sometimes, this can improve your connection speed.
- **Network Not Showing:** Ensure your Wi-Fi is enabled on your computer. You can toggle the Wi-Fi on and off through the network icon in the system tray.

By following these steps, you should be able to connect your Windows 11 device to the internet either wirelessly or through a wired Ethernet connection. As always, take your time, and don't hesitate to ask for help from a friend or family member if you run into trouble.

BROWSER BASICS: MICROSOFT EDGE, CHROME, OR FIREFOX

Once you have successfully connected your Windows 11 computer to the internet, the next step is to understand how to use a web browser to access the vast resources available online. A web browser is a software application used to locate, retrieve, and display content on the World Wide Web, including web pages, images, videos, and other files. As we continue, we will focus on three popular browsers: Microsoft Edge, Google Chrome, and Mozilla Firefox.

Understanding Web Browsers

Most computers come with a default web browser pre-installed, and Windows 11 is no exception, providing Microsoft Edge right out of the box. However, you might prefer using Google Chrome or Mozilla Firefox, both of which can be downloaded easily.

Microsoft Edge

- **Pre-installed on Windows 11:** Ready to use without any additional installations.
- **User-friendly Features:** Includes features like reading mode, voice reading, and easy access to favorites.
- **Safety and Security:** Offers tools to protect your privacy and data while browsing.

Google Chrome

- **Popular Choice:** Widely used around the world, known for its speed and efficiency.
- **Extensions:** Provides a vast marketplace of extensions to enhance functionality.
- **Sync Capabilities:** Allows you to use your Google account to sync bookmarks, histories, and settings across devices.

Mozilla Firefox

- **Emphasis on Privacy:** Known for strong privacy controls to help keep your information safe.
- **Customizable Interface:** Highly customizable with themes and extensions.
- **Performance and Memory:** Good balance of speed and efficient memory usage.

Navigating a Web Browser

Navigating a web browser involves a few basic elements:

- **Address Bar:** Here you type the web address or URL (Uniform Resource Locator) you wish to visit. For instance, typing www.google.com will take you to the Google homepage.
- **Back and Forward Buttons:** These allow you to go back to the previous page or move forward to the next one if you've already navigated back.
- **Refresh Button:** If a page doesn't load correctly, clicking this button can reload the page.
- **Home Button:** Takes you back to your home page, which can be set to your favorite website for quick access.
- **Tabs:** Allow you to open multiple websites in a single browser window. You can switch between them without opening new windows, keeping your desktop tidy.
- **Bookmarks:** Useful for saving web pages you want to return to easily.

Setting Up and Using Each Browser

Microsoft Edge

1. **Find Edge on Your Computer:** Click on the Edge icon on the taskbar or search for it in the Start menu.
2. **Set Up Your Home Page:**
    - Go to Settings by clicking the three dots in the upper right corner.
    - Under "On startup," select "Open a specific page or pages" and enter the URL of your favorite page.
3. **Bookmarking a Page:** Click the star icon in the address bar to add the current page to your bookmarks.

Google Chrome

1. **Installing Chrome:** Visit www.google.com/chrome and click "Download Chrome." Follow the on-screen instructions to install.
2. **Syncing with a Google Account:**
    - Click on the profile icon in the upper right corner, then "Turn on Sync," and sign in with your Google Account.

3. **Managing Extensions:**
   o Click the three dots, go to "More tools," and then "Extensions." Here you can browse or manage extensions.

Mozilla Firefox

1. **Installing Firefox:** Visit www.mozilla.org/firefox and click "Download Firefox." Follow the on-screen instructions to install.

2. **Adjusting Privacy Settings:**
   o Click the three lines in the top right corner, go to "Options," then "Privacy & Security" to adjust your settings.

3. **Using Add-ons:**
   o Click the three lines, go to "Add-ons and Themes" to find and install add-ons.

Troubleshooting Common Issues

- **Page Not Loading:** Ensure your internet connection is active. If it is, try refreshing the page or restarting the browser.

- **Browser Crashes:** Close other programs to free up memory, or consider restarting your computer.

- **Slow Performance:** Clear your browser's cache and cookies or consider removing unused extensions and add-ons.

By selecting a browser that fits your needs and learning its basic functionalities, you can significantly enhance your internet experience. Whether it's keeping in touch with loved ones, reading the latest news, or enjoying multimedia content, mastering your web browser is a key step in becoming proficient in navigating the digital world.

UNDERSTANDING SAFE BROWSING PRACTICES

Navigating the internet safely is crucial, especially in an age where digital scams and threats are rampant. Understanding safe browsing practices is an essential skill that will help you avoid unwanted surprises and protect your personal information. As you browse websites, shop online, or interact on social media, being aware of these practices ensures a safer and more secure online experience.

Recognize Secure Websites

When visiting a website, especially when you need to enter personal or financial information, you must ensure it's secure.

- **Look for HTTPS:** Before the web address in your browser's address bar, you should see "https://" rather than just "http://." The extra 's' stands for secure, indicating that the website encrypts data between your browser and the site.

- **Padlock Icon:** A padlock icon next to the web address also signifies a secure connection.

- **Website Credibility:** Check the website's domain name for obvious typos or unusual characters that seem out of place, as these may indicate a 'phishing' site attempting to mimic a legitimate one.

Use Strong, Unique Passwords

Passwords are your first defense against unauthorized access to your accounts.

- **Create Strong Passwords:** Use a mix of letters (both uppercase and lowercase), numbers, and special characters. Avoid common words or easily guessable information like birthdays.

- **Use Unique Passwords for Different Sites:** If a hacker gains access to one of your passwords, you don't want them to have the keys to all your accounts.

- **Consider a Password Manager:** These tools can generate and store complex passwords for you, so you don't have to remember them all. They only require you to remember one master password.

Update Regularly

Keeping your software up to date is crucial for protecting yourself against vulnerabilities that hackers could exploit.

- **Operating System Updates:** Whether you use Windows, macOS, or another system, enable automatic updates to ensure you receive the latest security patches.
- **Browser Updates:** Similarly, set your web browser to update automatically. This helps protect you against security issues and ensures the browser runs smoothly.

Be Cautious with Emails and Links

Phishing attacks, where scammers trick you into revealing personal information, often occur through email.

- **Verify Sender's Information:** Check the sender's email address carefully if an email looks suspicious, even if it appears to come from a known contact.
- **Do Not Click on Suspicious Links:** Hover over any link with your mouse cursor (but don't click) to see the linked address. If it looks strange or unfamiliar, do not click it.
- **Avoid Downloading Unexpected Attachments:** These can sometimes contain malware. If an attachment comes from someone you know, verify with them through another communication method before opening.

Utilize Security Software

Even the most cautious can occasionally slip, which is where security software becomes essential.

- **Antivirus Software:** This software protects against malware that can infect your computer, compromising your personal information or damaging files.
- **Firewall:** Your computer's firewall (or a hardware firewall built into your router) can block unauthorized access to your computer through the internet.

Regular Backups

Ensure your data isn't lost in the event of a computer problem or a security breach.

- **Regular Backup Schedule:** Use an external hard drive or cloud storage service to back up your important documents, photos, and other data.
- **Use Automated Tools:** Many systems offer automated backup options that can help you keep your data safe without having to remember to back it up manually.

Stay Informed and Educated

Understanding the latest online threats can go a long way in helping you guard against them.

- **Stay Updated on the Latest Scams:** Regularly read about the latest scams and security breaches. Many websites offer up-to-date information on the types of threats currently prevalent.
- **Educational Resources:** Consider watching tutorials or reading additional resources on safe browsing practices.

Practice Safe Browsing Habits

Your behavior online can significantly impact your security.

- **Log Out from Websites:** Especially after completing transactions or anytime you've logged into a service on a public or shared computer.
- **Be Wary of Public Wi-Fi:** Avoid accessing sensitive information or making transactions when connected

to public Wi-Fi networks. Use a virtual private network (VPN) if you need to access sensitive information in public.

Regular Audits

Periodically reviewing your online security practices and settings can help identify potential weaknesses.

- **Check Privacy Settings on Social Media:** Make sure you're sharing information only with people you intend to.
- **Review Account Activity:** Regularly review the activity on your online accounts to catch any unauthorized actions early.

By adopting these safe browsing habits, you ensure a safer online experience that maintains the integrity of your personal information and enhances your enjoyment of the vast resources available on the internet. Remember, staying vigilant and cautious plays a crucial role in securing your online presence.

BOOKMARKING YOUR FAVORITE WEBSITES

In your journey through the digital world, you'll likely come across websites that you find useful, entertaining, or necessary for frequent visits. Bookmarking these sites in your web browser is like placing a bookmark in a book, allowing you to easily open them whenever needed without remembering the complex addresses. This key feature enhances your browsing efficiency and keeps your favorite sites close at hand.

What is Bookmarking?

Bookmarking is a method to store and organize website links that you can easily access in future sessions. Think of it as creating a personalized list of shortcuts to your preferred websites.

Benefits of Bookmarking

- **Quick Access:** Navigate to your favorite websites without typing the URL each time.
- **Organization:** Categorize bookmarks into folders (like personal, news, shopping) for better organization.
- **Ease of Use:** Easily add, remove, or edit bookmarks as your preferences and needs change.

How to Bookmark Websites in Popular Browsers

Each browser has a slightly different way of bookmarking, but the core concept remains the same. Below, we cover the steps for Microsoft Edge, Google Chrome, and Mozilla Firefox.

Microsoft Edge

1. **Open Microsoft Edge:** Click on the Edge icon to start your browser.
2. **Navigate to the Website:** Type the website you want to bookmark into the address bar and press Enter.
3. **Add Bookmark:** Click on the star icon (favorites) located at the end of the address bar. A small menu will pop up.
   - Name the bookmark as desired.
   - Select "Add" or choose a specific folder to organize the bookmark.
4. **Managing Bookmarks:**
   - To view or access your bookmarks, click on the three dots in the top right corner and select "Favorites."
   - You can drag bookmarks to rearrange them or right-click for further options like delete or renaming.

Google Chrome

1. **Open Google Chrome:** Click on the Chrome icon to launch the browser.

2. **Visit the Desired Website:** Enter the web address in the top address bar and hit Enter.
3. **Create Bookmark:** Click the star icon on the right side of the address bar. A dialog box appears.
   o Name your bookmark and select the folder where you wish to store it ("Bookmarks bar" for direct access).
4. **Bookmark Management:**
   o Access your bookmarks by clicking on the three vertical dots and going to "Bookmarks" > "Bookmark manager." Here you can organize or edit your bookmarks.

Mozilla Firefox

1. **Launch Mozilla Firefox:** Start Firefox by clicking on its icon.
2. **Navigate to the Website:** Type the desired website's URL into the address bar and press Enter.
3. **Bookmark the Page:** Click the star icon in the address bar. Once clicked, it will turn blue to indicate the bookmark is saved.
4. **Edit and Manage Bookmarks:**
   o To organize your bookmarks, click on the library icon (books), then "Bookmarks" > "Manage Bookmarks."
   o Here you can create folders, move bookmarks into folders, or delete them.

Tips for Effective Bookmarking

- **Naming Bookmarks:** Give your bookmarks descriptive names so that you remember what they are for.
- **Regular Cleanup:** Over time, review your bookmarks and remove those that you no longer find useful.
- **Sync Bookmarks:** If you use multiple devices, consider setting up syncing your bookmarks across devices using your browser's syncing feature. This way, whether on your tablet, phone, or computer, your bookmarks remain consistent.

Troubleshooting Bookmark Issues

- **Bookmarks Not Saving:** Check that you have permission to add bookmarks and that your browser is updated.
- **Missing Bookmarks:** If bookmarks disappear, check if syncing is enabled or you might be logged into a different user account.

Creating Bookmark Backups

- **Export Bookmarks:** For added security, regularly export your bookmarks. This can typically be done from the bookmark manager and saves a file that can be imported back if needed.

Conclusion

Bookmarking is a straightforward but powerful tool to enhance your browsing experience, reducing the time you spend typing or searching for websites and making sure that essential resources are always at your fingertips. By taking a few moments to learn and utilize this feature, you'll find the internet more navigable and personalized to your needs.

6. EMAIL AND COMMUNICATION

SETTING UP YOUR EMAIL ACCOUNT

Setting up an email account on your Windows 11 computer is like getting a new address in the digital neighborhood. It allows you to send letters (emails) to anyone in the world within seconds, and receive responses just as quickly! This step-by-step guide will walk you through the process of setting up your email account, ensuring you remain connected with friends, family, and the world at large.

Step 1: Choose Your Email Provider

Before you can set up an email, you need to choose where your digital mailbox will be located. There are several free, user-friendly services available including:

- **Microsoft Outlook**
- **Gmail by Google**
- **Yahoo Mail**

These providers offer robust security features and are great for beginners. For this guide, we will use Gmail as an example, but steps for other service providers will be similar.

Step 2: Creating a New Email Account

Open Your Browser

1. Click on the Microsoft Edge icon on your taskbar (it looks like a blue-and-green e).

2. Type gmail.com in the address bar at the top of the screen and press Enter.

Start the Signup Process

1. You will see a page titled Create your Google Account. Click on Create account.

Google Account   Overview   Privacy Tools   Create an account

2. Select For myself from the options provided.

Fill in Your Personal Details

1. Enter your First name and Last name.
2. Choose a username — this will be your email address.
3. Create a password and re-enter it in the next box to confirm. Make sure your password is something secure that you can remember.

Complete the Signup Process

1. Click Next and fill in any additional required information such as your phone number or recovery email address (which is handy if you ever forget your password).
2. Proceed through the rest of the Google prompts, providing information and making selections as needed.
3. Finish by agreeing to Google's Terms of Service and Privacy Policy. Click Create Account.

Step 3: Accessing Your Email

Sign in to Your Email

1. If you are not automatically logged in, go to gmail.com again.
2. Enter your new email address and click Next.
3. Input your password and click Next.

Tour Your Email Inbox

Once logged in, you might see a welcome email from Google. Feel free to read this as it contains helpful information regarding using Gmail. Take a moment to familiarize yourself with the layout:

- **Inbox**: Where you'll find emails people have sent you.
- **Sent Mail**: Where copies of emails you've sent are stored.
- **Drafts**: Emails you've started writing but haven't sent yet.
- **Spam**: Emails that are not trustworthy, often unsolicited marketing emails.
- **Trash**: Deleted emails.

Step 4: Sending Your First Email

Compose a New Email

1. Find and click the + Compose button, usually located at the top left of your screen.
2. A new window will pop up.

Address the Email

1. In the 'To' field, type the email address of the person you're writing to.
2. Add a 'Subject' in the next field, which is a brief title for your email.

Write Your Message

1. Below the subject field is a large area where you can write your message.
2. When you're done, click the blue Send button at the bottom.

Step 5: Managing Your Email

Search for Emails

Use the search bar at the top to find specific emails.

Organize with Folders

1. You can create folders by clicking More on the sidebar and then Create new label.
2. Name your folder and click Create.

Adjust Settings

To tweak settings, click the gear icon in the upper-right corner and select See all settings. From here, you can change themes, configure inbox settings, and more.

Tips for Staying Safe and Secure

- **Strong Passwords**: Ensure your password includes a mix of letters, numbers, and symbols.
- **Sign Out**: Always sign out if you're using a shared or public computer.
- **Watch for Phishing**: Be cautious about emails asking for personal information, even if they look legitimate.

Remember, setting up and using an email doesn't just keep you connected; it ensures you can manage appointments, receive notifications, and even shop online. Take it one step at a time, and you'll find it a vital tool for your everyday tasks.

SENDING AND RECEIVING EMAILS

Learning to send and receive emails is like unlocking a gateway to modern communication, allowing you to connect with the people and discussions that matter most to you. This guide is tailored specifically for you to become comfortable and capable with these fundamental tasks using your email account in Windows 11.

Understanding the Email Interface

Upon logging into your email provider, you typically find a similarly structured interface:

- **Inbox**: Where all incoming emails are gathered.
- **Sent Mail**: Contains copies of all your sent messages.
- **Drafts**: Emails you've started but haven't completed or sent.
- **Spam**: Unwanted emails that are filtered out automatically.
- **Trash**: Where your deleted emails reside temporarily.

Sending an Email

Sending an email can be a wonderful way to share news, ask questions, or simply say hello. Let's break it down into simple steps:

1. **Open Your Email Client**
   - Either through a desktop app provided by your email service or by visiting the website of your email provider.

2. **Start a New Email**
   - Look for a button that might say New, Compose, or show a plus (+) sign.
   - This will open a blank email window.

3. **Address Your Email**
   - **To**: Enter the email address of the person you want to communicate with.
   - **Cc (Carbon Copy)**: Add addresses of other recipients who you want to see the message.
   - **Bcc (Blind Carbon Copy)**: Add addresses discreetly, without other recipients knowing.

4. **Write the Subject Line**
   - This is a brief headline that describes the purpose of your email. It helps recipients understand the importance and content of your email quickly.

5. **Compose Your Message**
   - Click in the large box below 'Subject' and type your message.
   - Make sure to keep your message clear and concise for easy understanding.

6. **Attach Files (Optional)**
   - If you need to send a document or photo, look for a paperclip icon or an option labeled Attach.
   - Click on it and select the file from your computer.

7. **Review and Send**
   - Before you hit send, review your email for typos or any added information.
   - Click the Send button once you're ready. It's often a button with an icon of an airplane.

Receiving an Email

1. **Check Your Inbox**
   - When someone sends you an email, it will appear in your inbox.
   - Refresh your inbox if you're expecting an email that isn't appearing.

2. **Open and Read**
   - o   Simply click on any email title to open and read it in full.
3. **Reply, Forward, or Delete**
   - o   To respond directly to the sender, use the Reply button.
   - o   If you want to include other people in your response, use Reply All.
   - o   To send this email to someone else, use the Forward option.
   - o   If you think you won't need the email anymore, you can press Delete to move it to Trash.

Organizing Emails

To maintain a clean and manageable inbox, consider these tips:

- **Create Folders**: Organize emails by creating folders for different categories, like family, receipts, work, etc.
- **Mark as Important**: Most email services allow you to mark emails that are of greater significance. Look for a star or similar symbol.
- **Regular Cleaning**: Schedule time to clear out your inbox, deleting or archiving emails that are no longer needed.

Security Practices

1. **Be Wary of Suspicious Emails**: Do not open emails from unknown senders, especially those that request personal information or prompt you to click on a link.
2. **Use Spam Filters**: Ensure your spam filter is activated in your email settings to automatically divert potential junk mail away from your inbox.
3. **Regular Updates**: Keep your email application or web service updated for the latest security measures.

Common Problems and Quick Fixes

- **Not Receiving Emails**: Check your spam folder, ensure you have internet connectivity, and verify the sender has the correct email address.
- **Attachment Issues**: If you can't open an attachment, ensure you have the necessary software installed on your computer.
- **Forgotten Passwords**: Use the 'Forgot Password' feature usually located at the login screen of your email provider's website.

With these steps and tips, you're well on your way to mastering the art of email communication. Each email is a learning opportunity, and with each one sent and received, you become more familiar with the digital world at your fingertips. This not only bridges the gap between you and distant loved ones but significantly broadens your horizons in the comfort of your own home.

VIDEO CHATS WITH FAMILY AND FRIENDS USING SKYPE OR ZOOM

In today's world, staying connected with your loved ones is more important than ever, and thanks to technology, it doesn't have to involve complicated setups. Video chatting apps like Skype and Zoom make it possible to see and interact with family and friends face-to-face across the globe. Let's explore how you can use these platforms to keep in touch, share moments, and even participate in gatherings from the comfort of your home.

Getting Started with Skype and Zoom

Skype and **Zoom** are popular video calling services that work similarly but have some distinct features. Choose the one that your family or friends use most frequently, or try both to see which you prefer!

Downloading and Installing the Software

1. **Open your web browser**: Use Microsoft Edge or any other browser.
2. **Visit the website**: Go to skype.com for Skype or zoom.us for Zoom.

3. **Download the software**: Find the download section on the website. For Skype, look for Get Skype, and for Zoom, select the Download under 'Zoom Client for Meetings'.
4. **Install the application**: Once downloaded, open the file (it usually appears at the bottom of your browser window or in your Downloads folder) and follow the on-screen instructions to install.

Creating Your Account

1. **Launch the application**: Open Skype or Zoom from your desktop or start menu.
2. **Sign up**: Select the option to create a new account. You will need to provide an email address and create a password. Follow any additional steps as prompted, including verifying your email address.
3. **Log in**: Once your account is created, use your new credentials to log in to the application.

Setting Up Your Device

Before starting your first video call, ensure your camera and microphone are set up correctly.

- **Check your camera**: You should see yourself when the video is enabled.
- **Test your microphone**: Speak into it and ensure the application is receiving the audio.
- **Adjust your speakers or headset**: Make sure you can hear incoming audio clearly.

Making a Video Call

1. **Add contacts**: You need to add the people you wish to call to your contact list in Skype or Zoom. You can search for them by their email address or username.
2. **Start a call**: Once you have added someone as a contact, select their name from your contact list and choose the video call button. It looks like a small camera.
3. **Enjoy chatting**: When the call connects, you'll see your friend or family member on screen! There are options on your screen to mute your microphone, turn off your video, and more.

Participating in Group Calls

1. **Initiate a group call**: Select multiple contacts from your list (hold down Ctrl while clicking to select more than one), and then choose the video call icon.
2. **Joining a call**: For Zoom, if you're given a meeting ID, you can join by selecting Join a Meeting and entering

the ID. Skype allows you to click on a link in your email or messaging app.

Tips for a Great Video Chat Experience

- **Good Lighting**: Position yourself where your face is well-lit, preferably with natural light.
- **Quiet Environment**: Reduce background noise so others can hear you clearly.
- **Internet Connection**: Use a stable and fast internet connection for the best video quality.

Trouble-shooting Common Issues

- **Audio Problems**: Check if the microphone is muted or the volume is too low both on your device and in the app.
- **Video Issues**: Ensure your camera isn't covered and is properly connected to your computer.
- **Connection Issues**: Restart the router if your internet connection is unstable or slow.

Additional Features

Both Zoom and Skype offer features that enhance video chats:

- **Screen Sharing**: Share your screen to show photos, documents, or navigate the internet together.
- **Recording**: Save memorable conversations with the option to record your calls.
- **Virtual Backgrounds**: Spice up your calls with virtual backgrounds in Zoom, which can change your background to a location or image of your choice.

Practice Makes Perfect - Don't worry if it takes a couple of tries to get everything right. The more you practice, the more comfortable you will become with these tools. Video chatting is not just about seeing each other; it's about sharing life's moments and staying actively connected. Whether it's a weekly chat or celebrating birthdays online, mastering video calls adds a valuable dimension to how you communicate with your loved ones, making each conversation a bit more special.

USING MICROSOFT TEAMS FOR GROUP CONVERSATIONS

Microsoft Teams is a powerful tool that not only facilitates group conversations but also integrates various functionalities to enhance teamwork and communication, especially fitting if you are involved in community groups, family gatherings, or collaborative projects. Its user-friendly interface caters well to those who may not have a lot of technical experience, allowing users like you to engage vividly and effectively with others. This guide will lead you through the basics of using Microsoft Teams for group conversations, ensuring you can connect and collaborate effortlessly.

Setting Up Microsoft Teams

1. **Download and Install Microsoft Teams**
   - Open your preferred internet browser and navigate to the official Microsoft Teams webpage.
   - Locate the 'Download for Desktop' button, choose your respective version (Windows or Mac), and follow the instructions to download and install the application on your computer.

2. **Create or Sign In to Your Microsoft Account**
   - Once Teams is installed, open the application. You will be prompted to either sign in or create a new Microsoft account. If you already have a Microsoft account (perhaps from using Outlook or Windows), use those credentials here; otherwise, you'll need to create a new one.

3. **Familiarize Yourself with the Interface**
   - Main navigation tabs (Activity, Chat, Teams, Calendar, Calls, Files) on the left sidebar.
   - The search bar at the top for quickly finding messages, people, or files.

- o Settings and options are accessible through your profile picture at the top right corner.

Starting and Managing Group Conversations

1. **Creating a Team**
   - o Click on the 'Teams' tab on the left sidebar, then select 'Join or create a team' at the bottom.
   - o Click 'Create team' from the choices. You can start from scratch or build from an existing group.
   - o Name your team, add a description if desired, and set privacy settings.
   - o Click 'Create' and then add members by entering their email addresses.

2. **Initiating a Group Conversation**
   - o Within a team, click on the 'Posts' tab to start a new conversation. Here you can type your message and then press enter to post it. Everyone in the team can see and respond to threaded messages.

3. **Scheduling a Group Meeting**
   - o Navigate to the 'Calendar' tab on the left, then click on 'New Meeting' at the top right.
   - o Add a title, set the date and time, select attendees by entering their email addresses, and add details about the meeting.
   - o Click 'Send' to send an invitation to all attendees.

Video Meetings and Calls

1. **Making Video Calls**
   - o From within any conversation, click on the video camera icon at the upper-right to start a video call with the group members.
   - o During the call, you can use various features like sharing your screen, opening chat, or adding more people to the call.

2. **Joining Calls**
   - o If someone starts a call, you'll see a notification in the team channel or be directly called. Click 'Join' to enter the call.

Utilizing Additional Features

1. **Sharing Files and Collaborating**
   - o You can share files in the 'Files' tab within a team channel. Just click 'Upload' and select the file from your computer.
   - o Collaborate on files in real-time, allowing multiple members to edit documents simultaneously.

2. **Using the Chat Feature**
   - o For more private conversations, use the 'Chat' tab. You can have one-on-one chats or group chats outside of a formal team setting.

Best Practices for Using Microsoft Teams

- **Stay Organized**: Use different channels within a team to separate discussions on different topics or projects.
- **Custom Notifications**: Adjust notification settings in Teams to control the frequency and type of alerts you receive to avoid being overwhelmed.
- **Regular Updates**: Since Microsoft often updates Teams with new features and security improvements, keeping the application updated ensures you have access to the latest tools and enhancements.

Security and Privacy in Teams

- **Manage Permissions**: Be mindful of who you add to meetings and what permissions you assign. Only share files with those who require access.

- **Use Strong Passwords**: As with any online tool, ensure your Microsoft account has a strong, unique password.
- **Be Cautious with Links and Files**: Do not click on suspicious links or download files from unknown sources within Teams chats or channels.

Microsoft Teams is more than just a platform for video calls; it's a comprehensive suite designed to facilitate easier and more effective communication and collaboration. Whether you're planning a family reunion, keeping up with friends, or coordinating a local book club, Teams offers the tools you need to keep everyone connected and engaged. With practice, it will become an invaluable part of your daily interactions, bringing the world closer to you from the safety and comfort of your desktop.

7. MANAGING FILES AND FOLDERS

UNDERSTANDING FILE EXPLORER

Imagine stepping into a well-organized library where every book has its place. This is much like using File Explorer in Windows 11—a powerful tool that helps you find, organize, and manage all the files and folders on your computer. Whether you're looking to organize family photos, manage documents, or find downloaded files, mastering File Explorer will make these tasks straightforward and less intimidating.

What is File Explorer?

File Explorer

File Explorer is the application in Windows 11 that allows you to navigate through the files and folders on your computer, just as you would sift through files in a filing cabinet. When you open File Explorer, you can view and manage the data stored on your computer or any connected external devices like USB drives.

Opening File Explorer

You can access File Explorer by clicking on its icon in the taskbar—it looks like a folder. Alternatively, you can press the Windows + E keys on your keyboard as a shortcut.

Upon opening File Explorer, you'll see a window divided into parts:

- **Navigation Pane:** On the left side, displaying folders like Desktop, Downloads, and This PC.

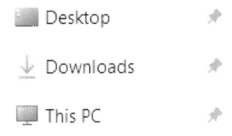

- **Main Window:** Shows the contents of the selected folder.
- **Address Bar:** At the top, allowing you to see the path of the current folder.
- **Search Box:** Located in the top-right corner for quickly finding specific files.

Understanding Important Sections of File Explorer

- **Quick Access:** This handy feature keeps your frequently used folders and recently accessed files at the forefront. You can pin folders here by right-clicking them and selecting "Pin to Quick Access".
- **This PC:** Shows drives such as your hard disk, connected devices, and folders like Documents and Pictures.
- **Downloads:** A default folder where files you download from the Internet are typically saved.
- **Network:** Check here to view other computers or devices connected to your home network.

Managing Files and Folders

Creating a New Folder

1. Navigate to the location where you want the folder.
2. Right-click on an empty space, select New, and then Folder.

3. Name the folder and press Enter.

Moving Files

To move files from one folder to another: 1. Find the file you want to move. 2. Right-click on the file and choose Cut. 3. Navigate to where you want to place the file, right-click, and select Paste.

Copying Files

Copying files works like moving them, but instead of choosing Cut, you select Copy. Right-click where you want to duplicate the file and choose Paste.

Deleting Files

To remove unwanted files:

1. Select the file by clicking on it.

2. Press the Delete key on your keyboard or right-click and choose Delete.

3. The file will move to the Recycle Bin until you empty it.

Searching for Files and Folders

File Explorer has a powerful search box located at the top-right. To find a file or folder:

1. Click into the Search Box.

2. Start typing the name of the file or keywords.

3. Results will appear as you type, filtering the contents of the current folder.

Customizing the View in File Explorer

You can change how items in File Explorer are displayed by using the options under the View tab at the top:

- **Icons Size:** Choose between large, medium, or small icons.

- **Details:** Display items in a list with details such as size, type, and modified date.

- **Group By:** Organize files by properties like date, type, or name.

Set your preferred view for each folder or apply it to all folders by selecting "Options" under the View tab and adjusting the settings in the Folder Options dialog.

Sorting and Grouping Files

Sorting and grouping can help you organize files more efficiently:

- To **sort** files, right-click in the blank space, hover over Sort by, and select criteria like name, date, or size.

- To **group** files, right-click, choose Group by, and select how you want to group the files, such as by type or date modified.

Tips for Efficient File Management

1. **Regularly backup important files** to an external drive or cloud storage.

2. **Rename files** and folders for easy recognition, by right-clicking them and selecting Rename.

3. **Use file compression** to save space. Right-click on a file or folder, select Send to, and then Compressed (zipped) folder.

By familiarizing yourself with File Explorer in Windows 11, you transform your computer into a well-sorted filing system that makes managing digital files not only simple but second nature. This understanding empowers you to use your computer more effectively, letting you focus more on what you enjoy and less on how to find or organize your files.

CREATING AND ORGANIZING FOLDERS

Organizing your electronic files into folders is akin to arranging physical documents into file cabinets. It's about creating a system where everything has its place, making it easy to locate and use. This section will guide you through the process of creating and organizing folders in Windows 11, ensuring that your digital filing system is as intuitive and manageable as possible.

The Basics of Folders

Folders in Windows 11 are containers where you can store and organize your files. Think of each folder as a drawer in a filing cabinet. You can have a folder for family photos, another for personal documents, and another for everyday tasks like bills or receipts.

Creating a New Folder

Creating a folder in Windows 11 is simple:

1. **Select the Location**: Navigate to where you want the new folder to be created. This could be on the Desktop, in Documents, or within another folder.

2. **Create the Folder**:
   - **Using the Right-Click Menu**: Right-click on an empty space, select New, then Folder. This creates a new folder in the chosen location.
   - **Using the Menu Bar in File Explorer**: Click Home at the top of File Explorer, then click New Folder. This places the new folder in the currently displayed directory.

After creating the folder, you should see it highlighted, ready for you to type in a name. Enter the desired name and press Enter.

Organizing Your Folders

Having a hierarchy of folders can help you keep everything organized. Think about how you categorize information:

- **By Type**: Create different folders for documents, pictures, videos, and music.
- **By Date**: If you work with files that are date-sensitive, organizing by year, month, or event can be practical.
- **By Project or Topic**: For specific projects, such as home renovations, trips, or hobbies, create a dedicated folder for each.

Creating Subfolders

To further organize your files, you can create subfolders within a main folder. For instance, within the "Photos" folder, you might have subfolders named "2023 Vacation", "Family Reunions", and "Nature Trips".

Renaming Folders

If you need to change a folder's name:

1. **Right-click on the folder**.
2. Select Rename from the context menu.
3. Type the new name and press Enter.

This can be useful if the purpose of a folder changes or if you made a spelling error when initially naming it.

Moving and Copying Folders

You might find that a folder is better suited in a different location, or you need a copy of it elsewhere:

- **Moving Folders**:
   1. Right-click on the folder.
   2. Choose Cut.
   3. Navigate to the new location.

4. Right-click on an empty space and choose Paste.

- **Copying Folders**:
  1. Follow the same steps as moving, but choose Copy instead of Cut in the first step.

Deleting Folders

If a folder is no longer needed:

1. Right-click on the folder.
2. Select Delete.
3. Confirm the deletion, if prompted.

Deleted folders go to the Recycle Bin and can be restored or permanently removed from there.

Useful Tips for Managing Folders

- **Frequent Review and Cleanup**: Just like physical files, digital folders need regular cleaning. Set a regular schedule to delete old or unnecessary files.
- **Use Descriptive Names**: Naming folders clearly and descriptively helps you and anyone else who might use your computer understand where to find specific files quickly.
- **Back Up Important Folders**: Regularly back up important folders to an external hard drive or cloud storage to prevent data loss.

By thoughtfully creating and organizing folders, you ensure that your digital work environment is as orderly and efficient as your physical one. Whether managing financial documents, personal photos, or general household information, a well-organized folder system makes finding and using data on your computer straightforward and stress-free. With these skills, you can maintain a tidy, logical digital space that complements your daily needs and activities.

MOVING, COPYING, AND DELETING FILES

Handling files on your Windows 11 computer involves a few key operations such as moving, copying, and deleting. These actions allow you to manage your digital documents similarly to how you might organize paper files in a drawer or folder. Let's break down these operations into simple, easy-to-follow steps.

Moving Files

Moving a file means transferring it from one location to another on your computer. This is useful when organizing your files or clearing space in a certain area of your computer.

1. **Open File Explorer**: This can be done by clicking the folder icon on your taskbar or by pressing Windows + E.
2. **Navigate to the File**: Go to the location where the file currently resides.
3. **Select the File**: Click on the file to highlight it.
4. **Move the File**:
   o **Drag and Drop**: Click and hold the file, drag it to the new location (open in another window or in the navigation pane), and release the mouse button.
   o **Cut and Paste**: Right-click on the file and select Cut. Navigate to the new location, right-click in an empty space, and select Paste. This method removes the file from the original location and places it in the new one.

Copying Files

Copying a file creates a duplicate of the file in a new location, while the original remains intact.

This is useful for creating backups or when you need multiple versions of a file in different places.

1. **Open File Explorer**: Use the folder icon on the taskbar or press Windows + E.
2. **Navigate to the Original File**: Find the file that you wish to copy.
3. **Select the File**: Click on it to highlight.
4. **Copy the File**:
   o **Drag and Drop**: Press and hold the Ctrl key, then click and drag the file to the desired location. Release the mouse button to drop a copy of the file there.
   o **Copy and Paste**: Right-click on the selected file, choose Copy, go to the destination location, right-click in an empty area, and select Paste. This leaves a copy of the file both in the original and the new location.

Deleting Files

Deleting files helps clear up clutter and free up storage space on your device. However, it's important to be sure you no longer need the file, as recovering deleted data can be cumbersome.

1. **Locate the File**: Open File Explorer (Windows + E) and navigate to the file you want to delete.
2. **Select the File**: Click on the file to highlight it.
3. **Delete the File**:
   o **Using the Keyboard**: Press the Delete key. Alternatively, press Shift + Delete if you want to permanently delete the file without sending it to the Recycle Bin.
   o **Using the Context Menu**: Right-click on the file and choose Delete. This moves the file to the Recycle Bin, where it stays until the Bin is emptied.
4. **Empty the Recycle Bin** (optional): To permanently remove all deleted files, right-click on the Recycle Bin icon on your Desktop, and select Empty Recycle Bin. Confirm the action if prompted.

Tips for Effective File Management

- **Back Up Important Files**: Before deleting or moving large batches of files, make sure you have backups for any important documents. Use external drives or cloud storage services to keep a copy.
- **Check Double Before Deleting**: Always review the files you are planning to delete and ensure they are not needed. Check the Recycle Bin once more before emptying it.
- **Use Shortcuts for Efficiency**: Learning keyboard shortcuts, such as Ctrl + C for copy and Ctrl + V for paste, can speed up your file management tasks.
- **Label Files Clearly**: When copying or moving files, ensure they are well-labeled so you know what they contain. This prevents future confusion and helps organize your digital space effectively.

By understanding and using these fundamental operations, you will be able to keep your digital files organized just as neatly as your physical ones, ensuring quick access and efficient use of your space on Windows 11. These practices not only help keep your computer organized but also enhance its performance by eliminating unnecessary clutter.

UTILIZING ONEDRIVE FOR CLOUD STORAGE

In today's digital age, safeguarding our important files and photos is more crucial than ever, and OneDrive offers a simple and secure method to do just that. OneDrive is a cloud storage service provided by Microsoft, integrated into Windows 11, allowing you to store files safely online and access them from any device, anytime, anywhere. Let's explore how you can utilize OneDrive to manage your files effectively.

What is OneDrive?

OneDrive is your personal online storage space in the cloud, provided by Microsoft. It is directly integrated with Windows 11 and Microsoft Office applications. When you save files to OneDrive, they are stored online on Microsoft's servers, which you can access from any device connected to the Internet.

Setting Up OneDrive

When you set up your PC with a Microsoft account, OneDrive is typically set up automatically. Here's how to check if OneDrive is ready to use or to set it up:

1. **Find the OneDrive Icon**: Look for the blue cloud icon in the notification area at the far right of the taskbar.
2. **Sign in to OneDrive**:
   - Click on the cloud icon, and a window will pop up.
   - If not signed in, you will be prompted to enter your Microsoft account details.
   - Follow the on-screen instructions to complete the setup.

Uploading Files to OneDrive

Storing your files in OneDrive not only keeps them safe but also makes them accessible across all your devices.

1. **Open OneDrive**:
   - Click the blue cloud icon on the taskbar. Select 'Open folder' to open your OneDrive folder.
2. **Upload Files**:
   - **Drag and Drop**: Open the folder containing the files you want to upload in another File Explorer window, and simply drag them into the OneDrive folder.
   - **Copy and Paste**: You can also copy files from their location and paste them into the OneDrive folder.
   - **Save Directly**: When saving files from programs like Word or Excel, you can choose OneDrive as the location to save your files.

Organizing Files and Folders in OneDrive

Organizing files in OneDrive is similar to organizing them on your computer:

1. **Create Folders**: Right-click in an empty space within the OneDrive folder, select New, and then select Folder. Give it a name that will help you remember what's stored in it.
2. **Move Files into Folders**: Drag and drop files into these folders or use the cut and paste method to move them.

Accessing Files Anywhere

One of the biggest advantages of using OneDrive is the ability to access your files from any device, anywhere:

- **On the Web**: Visit the OneDrive website (onedrive.live.com), and log in with your Microsoft account to access all your stored files.
- **On Mobile Devices**: Download the OneDrive app from your device's app store, and log in with your Microsoft account.

Sharing Files from OneDrive

OneDrive makes sharing files or folders with friends and family simple:

1. **Right-click the File or Folder** in the OneDrive folder.
2. Select Share from the context menu.
3. A pane will appear where you can enter the email address of the person you'd like to share with or generate a link that you can send via email or another method.

Keeping Your Files Secure

OneDrive offers several features to help keep your files secure:

- **File Versioning**: OneDrive keeps earlier versions of your documents for up to 30 days, useful for recovering from accidental edits or deletions.
- **Personal Vault**: For highly sensitive information, you can store files in the Personal Vault, which provides an extra layer of security.

Managing Storage Space

OneDrive offers 5 GB of free storage, with additional space available for a fee. To manage storage:

- **Check Storage Usage**: Click the OneDrive icon on the taskbar, then click 'Help & Settings', and select 'Settings'. Under the 'Account' tab, you can see how much storage you're using.

Tips for Effective Use of OneDrive

- **Regularly Update Your Files**: Ensure that the files and folders in OneDrive are up to date by dragging in new files and updating existing ones regularly.
- **Use the Appropriate Folder Structure**: Organize your files in a way that makes sense to you, similar to how you would organize paper files.
- **Back Up Important Files**: Besides using OneDrive, regularly back up crucial files to an external drive.

By integrating OneDrive into your daily computing habits, you ensure that your important files are secured, organized, and accessible wherever you go. This powerful tool simplifies managing digital information, making your step into the cloud as smooth as possible.

8. CUSTOMIZING YOUR COMPUTER

PERSONALIZING YOUR DESKTOP

Personalizing your desktop in Windows 11 is not just about making your computer look nice; it's about making it feel like home. This section will guide you through the simple steps to adjust your desktop's appearance so it's easier and more pleasant for you to use. You will learn how to change your wallpaper, alter the theme, and adjust the sounds your computer makes, all tailored to your personal taste and needs.

Changing Your Desktop Background

The desktop background, or wallpaper, is the image you see on your computer screen when all programs are minimized. Windows 11 provides a variety of beautiful, high-resolution images to choose from, or you can use a personal photo.

1. **Right-click on your desktop**: This means clicking your right mouse button while your cursor hovers over a free area of your desktop (not on an icon).

2. **Select 'Personalize'**: A menu will appear when you right-click. Click on the option that says 'Personalize'. This will open the settings window directly to the 'Background' settings.

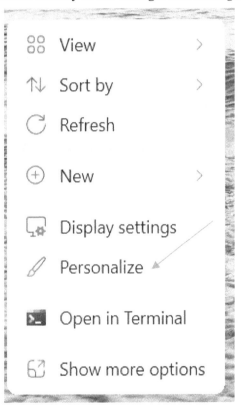

3. **Choose your picture**: Under the "Background" section, you'll see a preview of your current desktop background. Below the preview, you can choose 'Picture' and then either select a recent image or browse your computer by selecting 'Browse photos' to find the image you want to use.

4. **Adjust the fit**: Below the image selection, you can choose how the picture is displayed, such as "Fill", "Fit", "Stretch", or "Tile". Each option affects how your picture will cover the desktop.

Selecting a Theme

A theme is a set of coordinated settings including background, color, sounds, and cursor style. Windows 11 comes with several themes to choose from.

1. **Access themes**: Stay in the 'Personalization' settings from changing your wallpaper. Find 'Themes' on the

left side menu and click it.

2. **Preview and apply a theme**: You will see some themes listed here. Click on a theme to see a preview on the right. If you like it, simply click the 'Apply' button to change to this theme.

3. **Download more themes**: If you want more options, you can get more themes online. Click on 'Browse themes' which will redirect you to Microsoft Store's theme collection.

Adjusting System Sounds

Changing system sounds can be delightful. Maybe you prefer a softer, less obtrusive notification sound, or perhaps you find the default sounds unappealing.

1. **Open sound settings**: From the Personalization menu, click on 'Themes' and then select 'Sounds' (you may find this at the bottom of the theme settings or under 'Advanced sound settings').

2. **Explore sound schemes**: Windows categorizes sounds into 'Sound Schemes'. You can select an existing scheme or customize each sound. Click on each program event, like 'Calendar Reminder', and choose a sound from the list below it.

3. **Save your scheme**: After making adjustments, give your custom scheme a name by selecting 'Save As'. This way, you can easily switch schemes or revert any changes.

Adjusting Desktop Icons

Sometimes, the default icons on your desktop may be too small, too large, or not useful. You can change this:

1. **Right-click and personalize**: Right-click on the desktop, choose 'Personalize', then select 'Desktop icon settings' which is usually found at the bottom of the window.

2. **Change icon size**: If the icons are too small or too large for your liking, you can adjust their size by pressing 'CTRL' on your keyboard and scrolling your mouse wheel up to enlarge, or down to make them smaller.

3. **Choose which icons appear**: In the 'Desktop Icons' section, you can choose which common icons appear on your desktop, such as 'This PC', 'Network', or 'Recycle Bin'. Check the box next to each icon you want visible.

Consider Adding Widgets

Widgets on Windows 11 can give you at-a-glance information such as weather updates, news headlines, and more without opening your browser.

1. **Access widgets**: On the taskbar, you will find a widgets icon (looks like two small rectangles overlapping). Click this to open the widgets panel.

2. **Customize your widgets**: Click 'Add widgets' and choose from the available options like weather, family safety, or your calendar. You can also remove widgets by clicking the three dots in the upper right corner of each widget and selecting 'Remove widget'.

With these steps, Windows 11 allows you not just to use your computer but to make it a personal space where you feel comfortable and efficient. Customize it to suit your style and needs, knowing everything is just a few clicks away! Whether it's seeing your grandchild's smile every time you open your laptop or hearing a soothing sound when you receive an email, these personal touches can make a big difference in the enjoyment and usability of your desktop.

CHANGING THEMES AND BACKGROUNDS

Transforming the look of your computer can be both fun and fulfilling, providing a fresh feel every time you log in. Windows 11 makes it easy for you to customize themes and backgrounds, and this guide will show you exactly how in a few simple steps. By personalizing your computer, you not only make it more your own but can also make the screen easier to see and use according to your personal preferences.

Step 1: Accessing Personalization Settings

The journey to a new desktop look starts in the personalization settings. This is where Windows 11 keeps all the options for adjusting your screen's appearance from wallpapers to colors and themes.

- **Open Settings**: Click on the 'Start' button (the Windows icon typically at the bottom-left corner of your screen), then select 'Settings', which appears as a gear icon.

Settings

- **Go to Personalization**: Inside the Settings menu, you'll find various options. Click on 'Personalization', which is usually the first option in the second row, to start exploring background and theme settings.

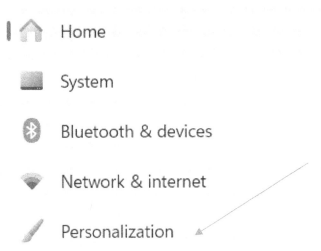

Step 2: Changing Your Desktop Background

Changing your desktop background is one of the quickest ways to refresh your computer's appearance.

- **Select Background**: In the personalization menu, 'Background' should be selected by default. If it's not, you can easily find it listed on the left side.

- **Choose Your Image**: You can select a picture from a preset list of Windows backgrounds or click on 'Browse photos' to upload an image from your own collection.

Personalization > Background

Picture

Solid color

Slideshow

| Windows spotlight   ⌄

○ **Personalize your background**
A picture background applies to your current desktop. Solid color or slideshow backgrounds apply to all your desktops.

- **Adjust the Fit**: Make sure your photo looks just right by ensuring its fit on the screen. You can select options like 'Fill', 'Fit', 'Stretch', 'Tile', or 'Center' to adjust how the image fits across your desktop.

Step 3: Choosing A Theme

A theme in Windows encompasses more than just your desktop picture. It includes the color scheme for your menus and taskbar, cursor appearance, and even system sounds.

- **Navigate to Themes**: You'll find the 'Themes' option on the sidebar within the 'Personalization' settings.

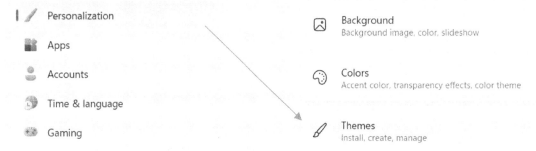

- **Explore Themes**: Windows 11 comes with several pre-installed themes you can choose from. Click on a theme for a preview. Choose the one that best fits your style.

Current theme   Windows spotlight ⌃
Choose a combination of wallpapers, sounds, and colors together to give your desktop more personality

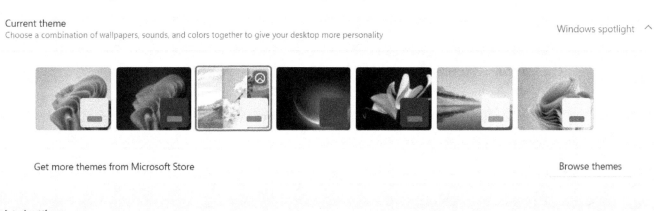

Get more themes from Microsoft Store   Browse themes

Related settings

☐ Desktop icon settings   ⬈

◑ Contrast themes   ⟩
Color themes for low vision, light sensitivity

72

- **Apply the Theme**: Once you have picked a theme, simply click on 'Apply', and it will change the overall appearance of your system immediately.
- **Get More Themes**: If the default options aren't suitable, go to the Microsoft Store by selecting 'Get more themes in the Store'. Here, you can download a variety of new themes.

Step 4: Customizing Colors

The color of your windows, start menu, and taskbar plays a big part in the look and feel of your PC.

- **Select Colors**: From the 'Personalization' menu, click on 'Colors' which is probably below 'Themes'.
- **Choose Your Color**: You can let Windows pull an accent color from your background, or you can pick a custom color. Scroll down further to choose specific places your color applies, like 'Start, taskbar, and action center'.
- **Contrast Themes**: If you find certain texts hard to read, you might consider trying out high contrast themes, which are designed to offer maximum visibility.

Step 5: Adjusting Transparency Effects

Transparency effects can give your Windows a subtle, elegant look by making the start menu, taskbar, and other background slightly see-through.

- **Find Transparency Settings**: Still in the 'Colors' setting, simply scroll down until you see 'Transparency effects'.
- **Toggle Transparency**: Turn this setting on by sliding the switch if it's off. You can turn it off in the same way if you find the effect distracting.

Step 6: Setting Your Lock Screen

Personalizing isn't just about what you see while using the computer but also when you start it up.

- **Access Lock Screen Settings**: Back in the 'Personalization' menu, click on 'Lock screen'.
- **Customize Your Lock Screen**: Choose your favorite picture or a slideshow for your lock screen. You can also adjust which apps show quick status and notifications on the lock screen.

These adjustments not only personalize your computing experience but can also help you navigate your computer more comfortably and efficiently. Each small change works together to turn the generic setup into a personal workspace that reflects your style and needs. Practice with different settings until you find a combination that feels right, simply knowing that it's easy to revert any changes or try new things anytime you like. Remember, this computer is yours to mold, and Windows 11 has provided the tools to ensure it can look and feel just right for you.

ADJUSTING SYSTEM SOUNDS AND VOLUME

Sound settings on your Windows 11 computer are not just about volume. They involve system notifications, multimedia playback quality, and the ease of hearing those distinct beeps and chimes that inform you of activity. Let's make sure you can hear what you need to, and none of what you don't, by adjusting system sounds and volume to your comfort.

Step 1: Accessing Sound Settings

To personalize how your computer sounds, start by accessing the sound settings where you can manage everything from volume levels to specific notification sounds.

- **Open Settings**: Click the 'Start' button (shaped like the Windows logo), then select 'Settings', represented by a gear icon.

- **Navigate to System Sounds**: In the Settings menu, click on 'System', and then select 'Sound' from the choices listed.

Step 2: Master Volume Control

Adjusting the master volume affects all sound output, which is useful for quickly turning sound levels up or down regardless of the application.

- **Adjust Overall Volume**: At the top of the 'Sound' settings, you'll see a slider under 'Output'. Dragging this slider left or right will decrease or increase the volume.

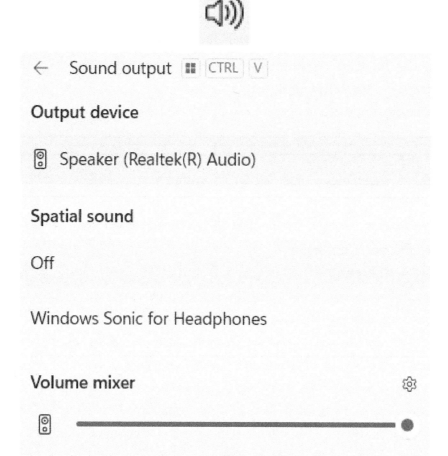

- **Test Speaker Output**: Click on the small icon next to the slider (usually a speaker icon) to play a test sound. This helps ensure your speakers are working and at a comfortable volume.

Step 3: Individual App Volume

Sometimes, certain applications or programs can be louder or softer than others. If you're having trouble with volume inconsistency, adjusting individual app volumes can be very helpful.

- **Find App Volume and Device Preferences**: Scroll down in the 'Sound' options and you'll see a section called 'Advanced sound options'.
- **Adjust Volume by App**: Here, you can adjust the volume sliders for each application independently of others. You can also choose different output devices for different apps, which is handy if you use multiple audio output sources.

Step 4: Changing System Notification Sounds

Notification sounds notify you about various system events like new emails, calendar alerts, or error messages. Customizing these can reduce confusion and improve the user experience.

- **Open Sound Settings for Notifications**: From the 'Sound' settings page, scroll down and select 'More sound settings'.
- **Customize Program Events**: In the 'Sounds' tab of the window that appears, you'll see a list labeled 'Program Events'. Here, you can select any event, such as 'New Mail Notification', and choose a sound from the list below it.
- **Test the Sound**: After selecting a sound, press the 'Test' button to hear it. If it's suitable, click 'Apply'; if not, try another until you find one that's pleasing and distinct.

Step 5: Creating Sound Schemes

Customizing sounds for various notifications can become your personalized sound scheme, which you can save and switch to anytime.

- **Save Your Custom Sound Scheme**: After modifying the sounds for different events, you can save these settings as a new scheme. Click 'Save As' at the bottom of the sound settings, and give your new scheme a name.
- **Switch Between Schemes**: If you wish to change back to the original settings or to another custom scheme, reopen the sound settings and select it from the 'Sound Scheme' dropdown menu.

Step 6: Reducing System Sounds

If you prefer a quieter computing environment, reducing or turning off system sounds may be beneficial.

- **Disable System Sounds**: In the 'Sounds' settings, you can select 'No Sounds' under the 'Sound Scheme'. This action turns off all notification sounds.
- **Control System Alerts**: You also have options to reduce the volume of system alerts specifically, independent of other sounds.

Adjustments detailed in these steps help you customize the auditory environment of your computer. This can not only make your PC experience more enjoyable and less disruptive but also ensure you are alerted to important notifications in a way that is most recognizable and least intrusive to you. Take some time to experiment with different sound settings; it can drastically change how you interact with and feel about your computer. Remember, you have full control over how these sounds play a part in your daily computer use, enhancing both the functionality and personal enjoyment of your technological experience.

9. APPS AND PROGRAMS

INSTALLING NEW APPS FROM THE MICROSOFT STORE

Embarking on the journey of discovering new applications (apps) can be both exciting and a bit daunting. However, the Microsoft Store on your Windows 11 computer simplifies this process. It provides a safe and straightforward way to find, install, and manage applications that can enhance your computing experience. Let's walk through the steps to use the Microsoft Store, ensuring that you can enjoy new apps with ease and confidence.

What is the Microsoft Store?

The Microsoft Store is similar to a digital shopping mall, where instead of clothes or household goods, you can browse a vast collection of software applications that range from productivity tools and games to news and weather apps. These apps are designed to run on your Windows 11 operating system seamlessly.

Accessing the Microsoft Store

To start exploring the Microsoft Store, you'll need to locate and open it:

1. Click on the **Start Menu** at the bottom-left corner of your screen.
2. In the list of pinned applications, look for the Microsoft Store icon; it looks like a shopping bag with the Windows logo on it. Click on this icon.
3. If you can't find it immediately, you can type "Microsoft Store" in the search bar at the top of the Start Menu and then click on the app when it appears in the results.

Navigating the Microsoft Store

Upon opening the Microsoft Store, you'll notice several sections that help organize content:

- **Home**: Discover featured apps and popular downloads right when you open the Store.
- **Apps**: Browse through categories like Education, Productivity, and Lifestyle.
- **Gaming**: Find games of various genres here.
- **Entertainment**: This is where you can find apps related to movies, music, and books.
- **Search bar**: Use this at the top of the window to look for specific apps by name.

Installing New Apps

Let's go through the process of finding and installing an app which can be incredibly useful. For this example, we will install a simple note-taking app called "OneNote":

1. **Use the Search Bar**:
   - Type "OneNote" in the search bar at the top of the Microsoft Store window.
   - Press **Enter** or click on the magnifying glass icon to search.
2. **Select the App**:
   - You'll see the "OneNote" app icon appear; click on it to go to its detailed page.
3. **Install the App**:
   - On the app's page, you'll see an **Install** button. Click it.
   - The installation will begin automatically, and you'll see a progress bar indicating the download and installation status.
   - Once installed, the **Install** button changes to **Open**. You can either click **Open** to start using the app immediately or find it later in your Start Menu.

Managing Your Apps

Once you install a few apps, managing them is key to keeping your computer organized and functioning smoothly.

Checking for App Updates:

1. Open the Microsoft Store.
2. Click on the **Library** icon at the bottom-left of the Microsoft Store window. This is where you can view all your downloaded apps.
3. At the top of this page, click **Get updates**. This checks for updates and installs them if available, ensuring your apps are current and secure.

Uninstalling an App:

If you find that you no longer need an app, here's how you can uninstall it:

1. Click on the **Start Menu**.
2. Find the app you want to uninstall in the list or type the name in the search bar.
3. Right-click on the app icon.
4. Select **Uninstall** from the contextual menu that appears.
5. Confirm by clicking **Uninstall** again in the confirmation dialogue box.

Tips for Safe and Effective App Management

- **Read Reviews and Ratings**: Before downloading an app, look at what other users say about it. This information can be found on the app's page under the description.
- **Mind the Permissions**: Some apps request permissions to access certain data or features of your computer (like your camera or microphone). Always review these permissions and only accept them if they make sense for what the app does.

Final Words

Exploring new applications can bring additional functionality to your computer and make your daily tasks more enjoyable or efficient. Remember, practice makes perfect. Each time you navigate the Microsoft Store and manage your apps, you'll become more confident in your abilities. Enjoy discovering what's in store for you in the Microsoft Store!

UNINSTALLING AND MANAGING APPLICATIONS

While exploring and installing new applications is quite thrilling, managing and occasionally uninstalling these apps is just as important for maintaining a tidy and efficient computer. This part will guide you through the steps of how to effectively manage and remove applications on your Windows 11 system, ensuring your device remains fast and responsive.

Understanding App Management

App management involves reviewing the applications you have, updating them regularly, and removing those you no longer need or use. Effective management can lead to better performance of your computer and a more organized digital environment.

Why Uninstall Applications?

There are several reasons why you might want to uninstall an app:

- **Freeing up space**: Apps can take up considerable space; removing ones you don't use can free up space for other files or apps.
- **Enhancing performance**: Some apps run background processes that can slow down your system, uninstalling these can improve your computer's speed.
- **Security reasons**: Occasionally, apps might become unsupported or could pose security risks if they are not regularly updated. It is safer to uninstall these apps.

How to Uninstall Applications

Uninstalling applications on Windows 11 is straightforward. Here's a simple, step-by-step guide to help you through the process:

1. **Open Settings**:
   o Click on the **Start Menu** button.
   o Select **Settings**; this can typically be found as a gear icon.
2. **Navigate to Apps**:
   o In the Settings window, click on **Apps** to open the apps and features settings.
   o This section will show you a list of all the applications currently installed on your device.
3. **Find the Application**:
   o You can scroll through the list or use the search bar at the top to find the application you want to uninstall.
   o Just start typing the name of the app, and it should appear.
4. **Uninstall the Application**:
   o Click on the app's name, and you'll see an **Uninstall** button appear. Click it.
   o A confirmation dialog might appear; click **Uninstall** again to confirm your action.
   o Follow any additional on-screen instructions if they appear.

5. **Check For Residual Files**:
   - Sometimes, apps leave behind data even after uninstallation. These can be found in the File Explorer, usually in the folder originally containing the app.
   - If you're comfortable, you can delete these leftover folders. If unsure, you might prefer to ask for help or leave them as they usually don't take much space.

Managing Applications

Apart from uninstalling, managing your apps ensures they function effectively and safely. Here are some tips on managing the applications on your Windows 11 device:

- **Regular Updates**: Keep your apps up-to-date. Updated apps offer new features, improved security, and better compatibility with your system. You can check for app updates through the Microsoft Store, or the app itself might automatically check for updates.

- **Startup Management**: Some applications are set to start automatically when you turn on your computer, which can significantly slow down your startup time. To manage this:
  - Go to **Settings**.
  - Select **Apps** and then **Startup**.
  - Here, you'll see a list of apps that can start automatically. You can toggle these on or off as per your preference.

- **Permissions Review**: Occasionally review what permissions your applications have. You can do this through:
  - **Settings → Privacy & security**.
  - Scroll down to find **App permissions** where you can manage what resources (like location, camera, microphone) your apps can access.

Tips for Healthy App Management

- **Review regularly**: Every few months, take some time to look through your apps and uninstall the ones you no longer use.

- **Be cautious with downloads**: Only download apps from trusted sources like the Microsoft Store to reduce the risk of installing malicious software.

- **Backup important data**: Before uninstalling apps, especially those used for work or that store your data, make sure to backup any important information.

Conclusion

Managing your applications is not just about keeping your computer tidy; it's also about ensuring it runs efficiently and remains secure. By regularly updating, uninstalling, and managing startup permissions, you can enjoy a smooth computing experience. Remember, a little regular maintenance can go a long way in keeping your digital life running smoothly.

EXPLORING DEFAULT APPS LIKE PHOTOS AND VIDEOS

Windows 11 comes with a suite of default applications designed to enhance your experience and productivity right out of the box. Among these, the Photos and Videos apps stand out for their ease of use and powerful features. These apps are crucial for managing, viewing, and editing your media files. This guide will introduce you to these apps, highlighting how they can enrich your digital life with Windows 11.

Using the Photos App

The Photos app is not just a tool for viewing images; it's a versatile program that allows you to organize, edit, and share your photos with ease. Here's how to make the most out of the Photos app:

Opening the Photos App

1. Click on the **Start Menu**.

2. Scroll to find the **Photos** app or type "Photos" into the search bar and press Enter.

Photos

3. Click on the app icon to open it.

Navigating the Photos App

Once opened, you'll see the main interface divided into several sections:

- **Collection**: Displays all your photos and videos, organized by date.
- **Albums**: Here, you can create and view organized albums.
- **People**: Uses facial recognition to group photos by the people in them (if available).
- **Folders**: View the folders on your computer that contain photos.

Editing Photos

The Photos app offers tools for basic photo editing:

1. Double-click on any photo to open it.
2. Click on the **Edit & Create** button on the toolbar.
3. Choose from options like **Edit** (to crop, rotate, or add filters), **Draw** (to draw on the photo), or **Create a video with text** (to make a simple slideshow).

Creating Albums

1. In the Photos app, go to the **Albums** tab and click on **New album**.
2. Select the photos you want to include and click **Create**.
3. Give your album a name and save it.

Using the Movies & TV App

The Movies & TV app is your go-to program for playing video files. It supports various file formats and offers tools for a smooth viewing experience.

Opening the Movies & TV App

1. Click on the **Start Menu**.

2. Search for "Movies & TV" in the search bar and press Enter.

3. Click on the app icon to open it.

Playing Videos

1. In the Movies & TV app, click on **Personal** to see your library of videos.

2. Click on any video file to start playing it.

3. Use playback controls like play, pause, skip, and volume adjustments located at the bottom of the window.

Managing Video Playback

- **Settings**: Access settings by clicking the three dots in the bottom right corner. Here, you can adjust playback speed, turn on captions, and more.

- **Mini player**: Click the small square icon in the bottom right corner to switch to a mini player, allowing you to watch your video while doing other tasks.

Tips for Getting the Most Out of Photos and Videos

- **Back up Your Media**: Consider using OneDrive or another cloud service to back up your photos and videos automatically. This protects your memories against hardware failures.

- **Use Keyboard Shortcuts**: Learn shortcuts like Spacebar (to play/pause), Arrow keys (to skip), and F (to full screen) to navigate quicker in the Movies & TV app.

- **Regularly Update Apps**: Ensure your Photos and Movies & TV apps are updated by checking the Microsoft Store for updates. This ensures you have the latest features and security enhancements.

Conclusion

The Photos and Movies & TV apps in Windows 11 are designed to make viewing, managing, and editing your media files a breeze. By familiarizing yourself with these tools, you can more effectively organize your digital memories and enjoy your multimedia content. Whether it's touching up a family photo to perfection or watching your favorite videos, these built-in apps support your needs without the necessity for additional software. Enjoy the process of learning these new skills at your own pace, and remember, each step you take is enhancing your capability to navigate the digital world.

10. MAINTAINING YOUR COMPUTER

KEEPING WINDOWS 11 UPDATED

Keeping Windows 11 updated is more than just a recommendation; it's essential for ensuring that your computer runs smoothly, securely, and efficiently. Microsoft frequently releases updates to improve the performance, add new features, and most importantly, enhance the security of your system. This sub-chapter will guide you through understanding what an update is, why it is important, and how to ensure your Windows 11 system stays up-to-date.

What is a Windows Update?

Windows Update is a service from Microsoft that delivers updates for the Windows operating system and associated Microsoft products. These updates can include:

- **Security fixes** that help protect your computer from viruses, spyware, and other malicious software.
- **Performance enhancements** that improve the overall speed and stability of your Windows system.
- **New features** that enhance your user experience and let you do more with your computer.
- **Driver updates** for better compatibility with devices like printers and scanners.

Why Update Your Windows 11?

1. **Enhance Security**: These updates close any vulnerabilities that might be exploited by malware or hackers.
2. **New Features and Improvements**: With each update, you get access to newer features as well as improvements to existing ones.
3. **Bug Fixes**: Updates often fix bugs that might be causing software crashes or other errors.
4. **Improved Compatibility**: They ensure that your system works well with new technologies and devices.

How to Keep Your Windows 11 Updated

Keeping your system updated might sound complicated, but it's quite straightforward with Windows 11. Here's how you can ensure your system is always up-to-date:

Step 1: Open Windows Settings

- Press the Start button.

- Click on the Settings gear icon, typically located on the lower left side of the Start menu.

Settings

Step 2: Navigate to Windows Update Settings

- In the Settings window, click on Update & Security.

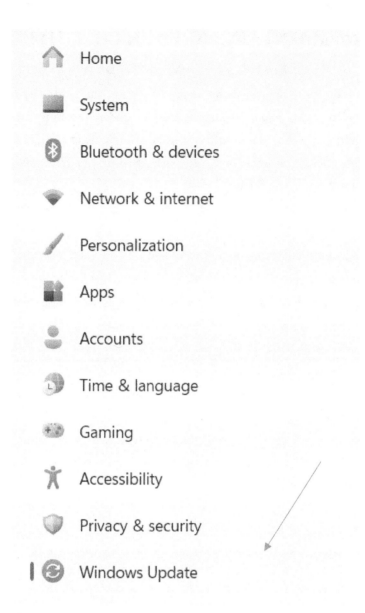

- Select Windows Update from the sidebar on the left-hand side.

Step 3: Check for Updates

- In the Windows Update section, you'll see an option to "Check for updates." Click on it.

Windows Update

You're up to date
Last checked: Today, 3:37 PM

Check for updates

- If there are any updates available, Windows will begin downloading them automatically.

Step 4: Install Updates

- After the downloads are complete, you might need to click "Install now" to start the installation process.
- Depending on the type of update, your computer may need to restart. Windows will inform you if a restart is necessary and often you can schedule it for a time that suits you.

Automatic Updates

Windows 11 is designed to make things as easy as possible, so it usually handles updates automatically. Here's what typically happens with automatic updates:

- **Automatic Download**: Updates are downloaded in the background without interrupting your work.
- **Active Hours**: Windows will respect your active hours (which you can set) where it won't automatically restart your computer to complete updates.
- **Restart Notifications**: Before restarting, Windows will notify you so that you can save your work. You can also snooze updates if needed.

Managing Update Settings

While automatic updates are convenient, you might want to have more control over when and how your PC updates. Here's what you can do:

- **Active Hours**: You can specify 'Active hours' in the Windows Update settings. During these hours, Windows won't restart your computer. This is particularly useful if you use your computer mainly in specific periods.
- **Paused Updates**: If you need uninterrupted use of your computer for a few days, you can pause updates temporarily. Go to Settings -> Update & Security -> Windows Update and select Pause updates for 7 days.

Troubleshooting Update Issues

Occasionally, you might encounter problems with updates, such as updates not downloading or installation errors. Here's how to troubleshoot:

- **Run the Windows Update Troubleshooter**: From the Settings -> Update & Security -> Troubleshoot -> Additional troubleshooters -> Windows Update.
- **Restart your Computer**: Sometimes, a simple restart can resolve the update issues.
- **Check for Storage Space**: Ensure your PC has enough space since updates require a certain amount to download and install.

Conclusion

Regular updates are vital for the health and security of your computer. They ensure that you have the latest security protections, new features, and performance improvements. By setting your Windows 11 to update automatically, you can enjoy a more secure, stable, and efficient computing experience without much effort. Remember, keeping your computer updated is a crucial step in maintaining your digital independence and staying safe online.

RUNNING VIRUS AND MALWARE CHECKS

In the digital age, maintaining the health of your computer involves vigilance against viruses and malware. These malicious programs can compromise your personal information, slow down your PC, and in worse cases, render it unusable. Regularly checking for and dealing with these threats is crucial, and Windows 11 has built-in features to help protect you.

Understanding Viruses and Malware

Before we dive into the strategies for protection, let's clarify what we're up against:

- **Viruses**: These are harmful computer programs that can replicate themselves and spread to other files or systems. They often disrupt the system's operation or damage files.
- **Malware**: Short for malicious software, it includes viruses, spyware, and any other software designed to harm your computer or privacy.

Both can arrive via email, downloaded files, or malicious websites. Recognizing the threat is the first step in protection.

Using Windows Security

Windows 11 comes equipped with Windows Security, a robust built-in tool that provides comprehensive protection against threats. Here's how to make the most of it:

Step 1: Accessing Windows Security

- Click the Start button and select Settings.
- Navigate to Update & Security and then choose Windows Security.

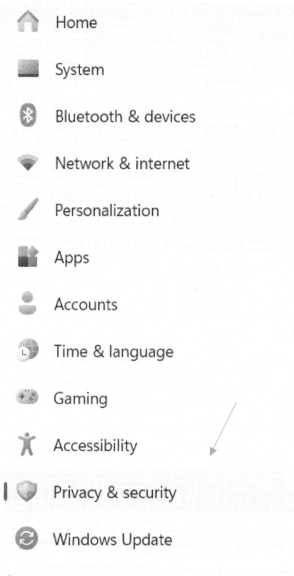

Privacy & security

Security

 Windows Security
Antivirus, browser, firewall, and network protection for your device

Step 2: Understanding the Security Dashboard

The Windows Security dashboard displays several protection areas:

- **Virus & threat protection**: Keeps checks on viruses, malware, and other threats.
- **Account protection**: Helps you manage user account access and settings.
- **Firewall & network protection**: Monitors network connections and controls who can send you data.

Privacy & security › Windows Security

Windows Security is your home to view and manage the security and health of your device.

Open Windows Security

Protection areas

Step 3: Running a Virus and Malware Check

- Under the "Virus & threat protection" section, click "Scan options".

Protection areas

- You'll see several types of scans you can perform:
  - **Quick Scan**: Checks folders where threats are commonly found.
  - **Full Scan**: Reviews everything on your PC.
  - **Custom Scan**: Lets you select specific files or folders to scan.
  - **Microsoft Defender Offline Scan**: Removes hard-to-find malware.
- Select the desired type of scan and click "Scan now".

Quick scan

Checks folders in your system where threats are commonly found.

Full scan

Checks all files and running programs on your hard disk. This scan could take longer than one hour.

Custom scan

Choose which files and locations you want to check.

Microsoft Defender Antivirus (offline scan)

Some malicious software can be particularly difficult to remove from your device. Microsoft Defender Antivirus (offline scan) can help find and remove them using up-to-date threat definitions. This will restart your device and will take about 15 minutes.

Automatic and Scheduled Scans

Windows Security is programmed to perform automatic scans. However, you can schedule your scans to ensure they don't disrupt your use:

Setting Up Scheduled Scans

- Go back to the "Virus & threat protection" settings.
- Look for "Virus & threat protection updates" and click on "Manage settings".
- Scroll to find "Automatic Sample Submission" and ensure it is turned on. This feature sends samples of suspicious items to Microsoft for analysis, improving protection.
- Under "Manage settings", you can also toggle the switch for periodic scanning to ensure regular checks even if you're using another antivirus program.

Keeping Your Antivirus Software Updated

The effectiveness of Windows Security depends on it being up-to-date. Updates usually occur automatically, but checking regularly ensures you are always protected:

- In the "Virus & threat protection" section, click "Check for updates" to download the latest virus definitions and software updates.

Best Practices for Avoiding Viruses and Malware

While Windows Security provides robust protection, your computing habits also play a critical role:

1. **Be Cautious with Emails and Attachments**: Don't open emails from unknown senders and be wary of attachments and links in unexpected emails, even from known sources.

2. **Use Strong, Unique Passwords**: For all accounts and especially for your PC login.
3. **Keep Software and Windows Updated**: As covered in previous sections, ensure all software and your operating system are up-to-date to minimize vulnerabilities.
4. **Use Secure Networks**: Avoid using public Wi-Fi for sensitive transactions, or use a VPN (Virtual Private Network) for better security.
5. **Back Up Your Data**: Regularly back up important files to an external drive or cloud storage.

If You Suspect a Virus or Malware Infection

If your PC is acting unusually slow, displaying frequent pop-ups, or behaving erratically, it might be infected. Here's what to do:

- **Run a Full Scan**: Using the steps outlined above, perform a full system scan.
- **Seek Expert Help**: If the problem persists, consider seeking help from professional computer repair services or Microsoft support.

Regular vigilance and understanding the tools at your disposal with Windows 11 will help keep your computer safe from various threats, ensuring you can use your technology confidently and securely.

BACKUP STRATEGIES FOR YOUR FILES

Ensuring the safety of your personal files and documents means more than just protecting your computer from viruses and malware. Regularly backing up your data is crucial to prevent loss from hardware failure, user errors, or theft. This sub-chapter will guide you through effective strategies to backup your files in Windows 11, allowing you to recover them if the unexpected happens.

Understanding the Importance of Backups

Before we discuss how to back up your data, it's crucial to understand why it's important:

- **Protection Against Data Loss**: Whether due to a malfunction, accidental deletion, or a ransomware attack, backups help you retain access to your information.
- **Ease of Recovery**: In the event of a computer failure, having a recent backup makes it much simpler and quicker to restore your system or set up a new machine.
- **Peace of Mind**: Knowing your important files are backed up provides confidence that you won't lose vital information.

Types of Backup Solutions

There are several ways to back up your data, each with strengths and tailored to different needs:

1. **External Drives**: Using an external hard drive or SSD (Solid State Drive) connected via USB.
2. **Cloud Storage Services**: Services like Microsoft OneDrive, Google Drive, or Dropbox, which store your data on remote servers.
3. **System Images**: Complete snapshots of your entire system, including settings, programs, and files.

Setting Up Backups with Windows File History

Windows 11 includes a handy feature called File History, which automatically backs up versions of your files to an external drive or network location. Here's how to set it up:

Step 1: Connect an External Drive

- Plug an external hard drive into one of your computer's USB ports.

Step 2: Configure File History

- Open Settings by clicking the Start menu and selecting the gear icon.

- Navigate to Update & Security and click on Backup.
- Under "Back up using File History", click on Add a drive and select your external drive.

Step 3: Choose Folders to Back Up

- File History defaults to backing up folders like your Desktop, Documents, Downloads, Music, Pictures, and Videos.
- To add more folders, click on "More options" under the Back up using File History section, then under Back up these folders, click Add a folder and select the folders you wish to include.

Step 4: Start the Backup

- File History will back up your files every hour by default. You can change this frequency under "More options".
- To perform a backup immediately, in "More options", click Back up now.

Using Cloud Storage for Backup

Cloud storage provides an offsite backup solution which protects your data from physical damage at home. Here's how to use it:

Step 1: Choose a Cloud Service

- Options include Microsoft OneDrive, Google Drive, and Dropbox. Windows 11 integrates seamlessly with OneDrive.

Step 2: Set Up Cloud Sync

- For OneDrive, you can find it pre-installed or download it from the Microsoft Store.
- Sign in with your Microsoft account, and select the folders you want to automatically sync.

Step 3: Access Files Anywhere

- Once set up, your files will be accessible on any device with internet access, providing an additional layer of convenience.

Creating a System Image Backup

For a more comprehensive backup solution, you can create a system image that includes your entire operating system, applications, settings, and all files:

Step 1: Open Control Panel

- Press Windows + S and search for Control Panel, then open it.
- Under System and Security, click on Backup and Restore (Windows 7).

Step 2: Create a System Image

- On the left, click the link Create a system image.
- Choose where to save the image (an external drive, DVDs, or a network location), and follow the prompts to complete the backup.

Routine Backup Checks

To ensure your data remains safe, periodically check your backup systems: - Verify that backups are completed successfully. - Try restoring a file from your backup to ensure everything is working correctly. - Keep your backup drives in a safe, secure place to avoid physical damage.

Conclusion

By setting up and maintaining regular backups, you can safeguard your valuable data and ensure that in any situation, from hardware failure to accidental deletion, you are prepared and protected. Remember, the time to think about backing up your data isn't after you've had a failure—it's before anything happens.

TROUBLESHOOTING COMMON PROBLEMS

Navigating and solving common computer issues may seem daunting, but with a bit of guidance, you can effectively identify and resolve many common problems that might arise with your Windows 11 PC. From unresponsive programs to issues with connecting to the internet, this section will provide straightforward steps to troubleshoot and fix these typical complications.

When Your Computer Slows Down

A slow computer can be caused by several factors, including too many programs running simultaneously, insufficient storage space, or outdated hardware. Here's how to address a slow computer:

1. **Close Unnecessary Programs**: Use the Task Manager (Ctrl + Shift + Esc) to close programs that are not needed. This frees up resources.
2. **Check for Updates**: Ensure your Windows 11 and all drivers are up to date. Updates can provide performance improvements and fix bugs.
3. **Run Disk Cleanup**: Search for 'Disk Cleanup' in the Windows search bar, select the drive you want to clean, and follow the prompts to remove unnecessary files.

When a Program Freezes or Crashes

Programs not responding can be a frequent annoyance. Here's what to do when a program freezes:

1. **Close the Program**: Press Alt + F4 to attempt to close the window or use Task Manager to end the task.
2. **Restart the Program**: Sometimes, simply restarting the program can resolve the issue.
3. **Update the Program**: Check if there are any updates available for the program, as updates can fix bugs that might be causing the issue.

When You Can't Connect to the Internet

Internet connectivity issues are common and can usually be resolved with some basic steps:

1. **Check the Wi-Fi Connection**: Ensure that Wi-Fi is turned on and you are connected to the correct network. Use the Wi-Fi icon in the taskbar to check your connections.
2. **Restart Your Modem and Router**: Unplug your modem and router, wait for about a minute, then plug them back in.
3. **Run the Network Troubleshooter**: Windows 11 includes a network troubleshooter that can automatically find and fix problems. Search for 'Troubleshoot settings' and select 'Internet Connections'.

When You Encounter Printing Problems

Printing issues might include the printer not responding or documents not printing correctly.

1. **Check Printer Connection**: Ensure that your printer is connected either via USB or over your network.
2. **Check for Printer Updates**: Keep your printer driver updated. Search for your printer model on the manufacturer's website for the latest driver.
3. **Restart the Printer**: Turn the printer off, wait a few minutes, and turn it back on. This can often resolve many minor printer issues.

When Windows Doesn't Start Properly

Sometimes, Windows might fail to start or frequently crash during use:

1. **Boot into Safe Mode**: Start your PC in Safe Mode to run only essential services. Press Shift while you click "Restart" from the sign-in screen to enter Safe Mode.
2. **System Restore**: If Safe Mode works, try using System Restore to roll back your computer settings to a previous date when everything was working fine.

3. **Reset Your PC**: If other options fail, consider resetting Windows 11. Go to Settings -> Update & Security -> Recovery, and select 'Reset this PC'. Be sure to back up your data first.

General Tips for Troubleshooting

These additional tips can help you with a range of other issues:

- **Keep Your System Clean**: Regularly removing dust from your computer, especially the fans and vents, can prevent overheating and performance issues.

- **Use Built-in Help**: Windows 11 offers searchable help files that can offer guidance on various features and settings.

- **Check the Cables**: Sometimes, simply reseating a cable can solve a hardware issue.

Conclusion

With these strategies, you can tackle some of the most common PC problems that you might encounter. Remember, regular maintenance like updating software, checking for viruses, and cleaning your system can prevent many issues before they start. If a problem persists or is beyond your comfort zone, don't hesitate to seek professional help. Advanced issues, particularly hardware related, may require a technician's expertise. By staying proactive and informed, you can enjoy a smooth, trouble-free computing experience with your Windows 11 PC.

11. STAYING SAFE ONLINE
UNDERSTANDING WINDOWS SECURITY FEATURES

In the digital age, your security online is paramount, especially as you venture into the new and vibrant world of Windows 11. Microsoft has worked diligently to weave robust security features into Windows 11 to protect your information and give you peace of mind while you explore, learn, and connect online.

Understanding Windows Security Features

Windows 11 comes with several built-in security measures designed to safeguard your computer from a variety of threats, including viruses, malware, and unauthorized access. Here's an overview of these features tailored to help you comfortably and safely navigate this new environment:

Windows Defender Antivirus

Think of Windows Defender as your personal security guard that constantly scans your computer for unwanted guests. It automatically checks programs you open, downloads new definitions from Windows Update, and provides an interface you can use for more detailed scanning options. Here's what it does for you:

- **Real-time protection:** This means it continually scans for malware, viruses, and other threats in real time.
- **Cloud-delivered protection:** Swiftly updated security intelligence means you're always protected from the newest threats out there.
- **Tamper Protection:** This feature prevents malicious applications from changing key security settings.

Firewall & Network Protection

A firewall is like a gated fence around your internet connection – it helps block hackers, viruses, and worms from reaching your device over the internet. Here is how the Windows 11 firewall keeps you safe:

- **Monitors traffic:** The firewall examines data coming in and going out of your network and blocks potential threats.
- **Network privacy settings:** Manage the privacy settings for different network types (public, private, or domain) so you can have stronger security in more vulnerable networks like public Wi-Fi.

Windows Hello and Secure Sign-In

Sometimes, passwords aren't enough to protect your accounts. Windows Hello offers a more personal and secure way to unlock your device. Here are the benefits:

- **Biometrics:** Use your face or fingerprint to access your device, which is much more difficult for someone else to replicate compared to a traditional password.
- **Hardware-based authentication:** Provides additional security layers beyond what typical password sign-ins can offer.

Device Encryption

Just as you might keep your important papers in a safe, device encryption helps protect your personal data by encoding it. If you lose your computer or it gets stolen, the encrypted data is much harder to access. Here's how it works:

- **Turn it on:** Device encryption is available on most Windows devices, and turning it on is simple through your settings.
- **BitLocker:** For more advanced control, Windows 11 Professional editions offer BitLocker encryption, which provides even stronger security options.

Internet Protection

Windows 11 includes settings and features to make browsing the web safer. Here are a few key components:

- **Microsoft Edge:** The new edge browser comes with security settings like Tracking Prevention, SmartScreen, and potentially unwanted app blocking, designed to keep risky and malicious web pages at bay.
- **Wi-Fi security:** Provides notifications about the security of Wi-Fi networks to ensure you connect safely.

Find My Device

Much like the feature available in smartphones, Windows 11 allows you to track your device's location in case it's lost or stolen. Setting this up means you can potentially retrieve your device or at least keep your data locked:

- **Location tracking:** Activate it to see your device's location history.
- **Lock it remotely:** If your device is lost, you can lock it remotely, securing your data.

Security Management

Windows makes it easy to monitor and manage your security settings. Here's how you can keep tabs on your protection:

- **Windows Security app:** Central place in your system where you can check your device's health and view or adjust security settings.
- **Security notifications:** Windows will alert you if there's something you need to address, so you never miss an important security update.

Regular Updates and Patches

Finally, keeping your system updated is crucial in protecting it against newly discovered threats and vulnerabilities. Windows 11 simplifies this:

- **Automatic updates:** Set your device to handle updates automatically, ensuring you're always up to date without having to worry about it.
- **Pause updates:** If you need not to update immediately, Windows allows you to pause updates for a set period.

Secure and Comfortable Online Experience

Navigating the internet securely can be a daunting task, especially with the evolution of threats and continuous technological advancements. But with Windows 11's security features, you have a sturdy foundation to protect your personal information and use your computer with confidence.

By understanding and utilizing these tools, you can enjoy a more secure online existence, knowing you're well-guarded by some of the most advanced features available today. Remember, the key to maintaining security is not just about having the tools but also about staying informed and conscious of potential threats, allowing you to navigate your digital life safely and confidently.

CREATING STRONG PASSWORDS

In today's digital age, where personal information is increasingly stored and managed online, creating strong passwords is paramount for your safety and security. A strong password acts much like a robust lock on the front door of your home, deterring intruders and protecting your private data. Let's dive into the essential aspects of crafting secure passwords to ensure your online experiences are as safe as possible.

Why Strong Passwords Matter

Strong passwords are your first line of defense against cyber threats such as hacking and identity theft. Hackers use various methods like brute-force attacks (trying many passwords very quickly), dictionary attacks (using common words and phrases), and phishing (tricking you into revealing your credentials). A solid password reduces your vulnerability to these attacks.

Characteristics of a Strong Password

Here's what makes a password strong:

- **Length:** Aim for at least 12 characters. Longer passwords are harder for thieves to crack.
- **Complexity:** Include a mix of uppercase letters, lowercase letters, numbers, and symbols.
- **Unpredictability:** Avoid predictable patterns and sequences, such as "1234" or "abcd".
- **Uniqueness:** Use a different password for each of your accounts. If one password is compromised, others remain secure.

Strategies for Creating Strong Passwords

Creating a password that is both strong and memorable might seem challenging, but these strategies can help:

1. **Use a passphrase:** Combine multiple unrelated words to create a long and complex password. For example, "BlueDaisySunset30!" is much better than "sunshine".
2. **Incorporate personal touch:** Think of a phrase or lyric from a favorite song or book, then modify it with numbers and symbols. For example, "Time_GoesBySo!Slowly1980".
3. **Include numbers and symbols meaningfully:** Replace letters with numbers or symbols in a way that is memorable to you. For example, the word "love" can become "L0v3".
4. **Utilize acronyms or initialisms:** Create a password from the first letters of each word in a sentence or phrase. For example, "My first house was on Maple Street in 2005" might become "MfhwoMSi2005!"

Tools for Managing Your Passwords

It's important not to reuse passwords across multiple sites. This is where password management tools come in handy:

- **Password managers:** Tools like LastPass, Dashlane, or 1Password can create and store complex passwords for you. You only need to remember one master password.
- **Two-factor authentication (2FA):** Enable 2FA wherever possible. This adds an additional layer of security by requiring not only a password but also a second factor like a text message code or fingerprint before access is granted.

Tips for Keeping Your Passwords Secure

Even the strongest password can be compromised if not handled properly. Here are some tips to keep your passwords secure:

- **Avoid sharing your passwords:** Do not share your passwords with anyone. If you must share access to an account, try to find a way to give them their own login credentials.
- **Be cautious of phishing scams:** Be mindful of emails or messages that urge you to click on a link or provide personal information.
- **Regularly update your passwords:** While you don't need to change your passwords too frequently, updating them regularly, especially if you suspect a breach, is advisable.
- **Monitor account activity:** Keep an eye on your account activities for any unauthorized actions that could indicate your password has been compromised.

Additional Layers of Protection

It's essential to consider additional protections on top of strong passwords:

- **Security questions:** Choose security questions and answers that are not easily guessed. Avoid common questions like the name of your first pet or the street you grew up on if this information is publicly available or shared.

- **Private browsing:** When using shared or public computers, use the private or incognito mode in your browser to avoid saving your browsing history and personal data.
- **Secure Wi-Fi connections:** Avoid using public Wi-Fi for transactions or actions that require logging into accounts. Use a virtual private network (VPN) if necessary to encrypt your connection.

Creating strong passwords does not have to be an overwhelming chore. With the right techniques and tools, you can generate passwords that protect your online presence effectively while also being easy for you to recall. Remember, investing a little extra time in crafting and managing your passwords can save you from potential cyber headaches in the future. Your digital security is worth that effort. Consider your newfound knowledge as a key to more secure and confidence-filled navigation through the digital world.

RECOGNIZING PHISHING SCAMS AND THREATS

Phishing is a type of online scam where criminals impersonate legitimate organizations via email, text message, advertisement, or other means to steal sensitive information. This technique is perversely simple and highly effective unless you know the signs to look out for. Understanding and recognizing these threats can help you navigate online safely, ensuring you maintain control over your personal data.

What is Phishing?

Phishing attacks involve tricking you into giving out personal information such as your bank account numbers, passwords, and credit card numbers. This is often done by sending messages that appear to be from a trustworthy source but are, in fact, crafted to deceive you into compromising your data.

Common Signs of Phishing

1. **Suspicious Sender Addresses:**
   - **Check the email address carefully.** Legitimate emails from companies should come from an address that matches the company's domain (like @companyname.com).
   - **Beware of slight alterations.** Phishers often subtly change email addresses (e.g., @companynarme.com instead of @companyname.com).

2. **Urgency and Fear Tactics:**
   - **Immediate action required:** Phishing messages often claim that urgent action is required to prevent something undesirable (like account closure or legal action).
   - **Threats and consequences:** The message might threaten severe consequences if you do not provide sensitive information immediately.

3. **Unsolicited Requests for Information:**
   - Phishing messages often ask you to verify or update personal information when there is no legitimate reason to request such data.
   - Be wary of any communication that asks for your password, credit card information, social security numbers, or other personal details.

4. **Links in Emails:**
   - Hover over any links (without clicking) to see where they really lead. Beware if the URL does not lead to the official website of the company that it claims to represent.
   - **Mismatched URLs:** Sometimes, the link text and the actual URL will differ.

5. **Spelling and Grammar Errors:**
   - **Professional communications are well-edited:** Mistakes in spelling and grammar can be a key indicator of phishing attempts.
6. **Attachments:**
   - Be cautious of email attachments, particularly from unknown senders. These can contain malware designed to infect your computer.

How to Respond to Phishing Attempts

- **Do not respond or click on links and attachments from unknown or suspicious sources.** This action alone can significantly reduce your risk of falling victim to a phishing scam.
- **Contact the company directly using a trusted method.** If a message from a company you do business with is asking for personal info, call them via a verified number to confirm the request.
- **Use security software and keep it up to date.** This software can often detect and alert you to risks before harm is done.
- **Educate yourself and others.** Awareness is a powerful tool against phishing.

Protecting Yourself with Technology

- **Email Filters:** Use email security features that can filter out many phishing attempts automatically.
- **Two-Factor Authentication (2FA):** As mentioned in previous chapters, setting up 2FA adds an additional layer of security.
- **Security Updates:** Regularly update your software and devices to protect against known vulnerabilities.

What to Do if You Fall Victim to Phishing

- **Change compromised passwords immediately.** This applies not just to the violated service but to any account where you've used the same password.
- **Notify the affected companies and your bank.** This can prevent financial loss and related complications.
- **Report the phishing attempt.** Inform the Federal Trade Commission via their website: www.ftc.gov, or forward the email to reportphishing@apwg.org. If the phishing attempt was a text message, forward it to SPAM (7726).

Understanding how to spot and respond to phishing attempts empowers you to use the internet with confidence. Phishing might seem daunting because it preys on human error, but with the right knowledge and tools, you can enhance your defenses against it. Remember, vigilance and skepticism are vital when dealing with unexpected digital communications. Be cautious, and remember the red flags discussed, you'll be well equipped to spot most attempts to compromise your online safety.

PRIVACY SETTINGS AND PROTECTING YOUR DATA

In the digital realm, your personal data is as valuable as any physical asset, and protecting it is crucial. Windows 11 provides robust tools and settings to help safeguard your privacy. Understanding how to adjust these settings is key to maintaining your digital autonomy and safety. Let's explore how you can manage these settings to secure your personal information effectively.

Importance of Privacy Settings

Privacy settings in Windows 11 help you control who can see and use your personal information. From location tracking to camera access, you can manage permissions for various applications and system operations, ensuring that only required data is shared or accessed.

Accessing Privacy Settings

To begin protecting your data, you need to know how to access the privacy settings:

1. **Open Settings:** Click on the Start menu, then select the settings gear icon, or simply press Windows + I on your keyboard.

2. **Navigate to Privacy & Security:** This section is dedicated to various privacy configurations, from general privacy options to app-specific permissions.

Key Privacy Settings to Adjust

- **General Privacy Settings:**
  - **Diagnostics & feedback:** Minimize the data you send to Microsoft by choosing basic settings.
  - **Activity history:** Disable this to prevent Windows from storing a history of activities on your PC.

- **Camera and Microphone:**
  - **Manage permissions:** Ensure that only apps you trust have access to your camera and microphone. Toggle access on or off based on your usage.

- **Location Services:**
  - **Control location access:** Turn off location services completely or select which apps can access your device's location. Remember, disabling this may affect apps like Maps or Weather.

- **Account Information:**
  - **Choose which apps can access your name, picture, and other account info:** This setting is crucial for protecting your identity.

- **Contacts, Calendars, and Other Devices:**
  - **Decide which apps can access your contacts and calendars:** This prevents applications from unnecessarily accessing and potentially sharing your contacts and calendar events.
  - **Connected devices:** Manage permissions for devices connected to your computer, such as phones or smart home devices.

Using Windows Security for Enhanced Privacy

Windows Security (formerly Windows Defender) is not only about protecting your PC from malware but also about ensuring your privacy. Here's how Windows Security can help:

- **Windows Security app:** Regularly check this app for health reports and take action on any recommendations that might affect your privacy.

- **Firewall & network protection:** This ensures external attacks do not breach your system, indirectly protecting your data.

Regularly Update Privacy Settings

Technology and applications are continually evolving, and so should your settings:

- **Check for updates:** Regularly reviewing and updating your privacy settings is vital as new features or updates can reset or create new privacy options.

- **Stay informed:** Keep up-to-date with new privacy features and settings introduced in Windows updates or by applications you use.

Best Practices for Overall Data Protection

- **Use strong passwords and authentication:** As covered in prior sections, strong, unique passwords and, where possible, two-factor authentication protect your accounts.

- **Be wary of phishing and scams:** Recognize attempts to steal your personal info. Your awareness can prevent most breaches.
- **Regular backups:** Regularly back up your personal data. Whether in the cloud or on an external drive, backups can save crucial information in case of a privacy breach.

Educating Yourself and Others

Part of protecting your privacy is understanding the risks and the tools at your disposal. Here are a few ways to stay educated:

- **Read about privacy:** Regularly read articles and news about privacy issues and protection strategies.
- **Use trusted sources:** Always use reliable, well-known security resources to gather information or download software.
- **Community learning:** Engage in community forums or groups to learn about others' experiences and solutions with privacy protection.

Your active participation in managing your privacy settings protects you from unwanted intrusions and potential data misuse. By taking control of the privacy settings in Windows 11, you not only safeguard your own personal information but you also contribute to a safer online environment for everyone. Equip yourself with the knowledge to confidently navigate the extensive capabilities of Windows 11, empowering you to use your computer with freedom and security.

12. ADVANCED FEATURES FOR SENIORS

USING VOICE ASSISTANTS: MEET CORTANA

Welcoming you to the world of voice assistants can feel like stepping into the future—a future where technology lends a helping hand in ways that are both practical and surprisingly simple. One such assistant is Cortana, built into your Windows 11 system, ready to make daily tasks smoother and more enjoyable. Let's explore how Cortana can be your digital companion, aiding you with everything from reminders to real-time information, all through simple voice commands.

What is Cortana?

Cortana is Microsoft's intelligent personal assistant. Think of it as a virtual helper living inside your computer, designed to assist you by answering questions, performing tasks, and managing your calendar, among other capabilities. Utilizing voice recognition technology, Cortana can understand natural speech patterns, meaning you can speak to it just like you would to a person.

Activating Cortana

To start using Cortana, you need to first enable it on your Windows 11 device. Here's a straightforward step-by-step guide on how to activate Cortana:

1. **Open Cortana**:
   o   Click on the Start Menu.
   o   Type 'Cortana' in the search bar.

Cortana

   o   Select the Cortana application from the search results.

2. **Sign In**:
   o   You'll need to sign in with your Microsoft Account. If you don't have one, you'll be guided on how to create a new account.

3. **Set Up Microphone**:
   o   Follow the on-screen instructions to set up your microphone, ensuring Cortana can hear you.

4. **Voice Activation**:
   o   You can choose to activate Cortana with a voice command by simply saying "Cortana," followed by your request.

How to Use Cortana

Using Cortana is as simple as speaking a command or question. However, knowing what you can ask will help you make the most of this technology. Here are some ways you can utilize Cortana.

Manage Your Calendar

- **Set Reminders**: "Hey Cortana, remind me to call John at 4 PM tomorrow."
- **Add Events**: "Hey Cortana, add a family reunion event on July 5th."

Get Answers to Queries

- **Weather Updates**: "Hey Cortana, what's the weather like today?"
- **General Knowledge**: "Hey Cortana, who is the President of France?"

Control Your Smart Home Devices

- **Adjust Settings**: "Hey Cortana, turn down the thermostat."

Launch Applications

- **Open Programs**: "Hey Cortana, open Microsoft Word."

Tips for Interacting with Cortana

To enhance your experience with Cortana, consider these helpful tips:

- **Speak Clearly**: Cortana works best when it can clearly understand what you are saying. Speak at a moderate pace and enunciate your words.
- **Be Specific**: The more specific your commands, the more accurately Cortana can assist you.
- **Use Natural Language**: There's no need for robotic commands; Cortana is designed to understand everyday language.

Privacy Concerns

Understanding how Cortana uses your data is vital. Here's what you need to know about privacy:

- **Data Usage**: Cortana collects data to personalize responses and recommendations. However, you can control what information Cortana accesses.
- **Managing Settings**: Access privacy settings directly in the Cortana dashboard to review and manage your data preferences.
- **Data Review and Deletion**: You can view the data collected by Cortana and delete it if desired, ensuring your information remains private.

Troubleshooting Common Issues

If you find Cortana is not responding as expected, here are a few troubleshooting tips:

1. **Check Microphone Settings**: Ensure your microphone is set up and functioning properly.
2. **Review Language Settings**: Cortana works best with certain language settings; make sure these align with your preferences.
3. **Update Windows 11**: Keeping your system updated ensures that all features, including Cortana, work efficiently.

Wrapping Up

Embracing Cortana in your everyday life can open up a world of convenience and connection. From sending emails to finding information online, this intelligent assistant is here to help you navigate your digital environment effortlessly. Remember, the more you use Cortana, the more attuned it becomes to your preferences and speech patterns, enhancing its ability to serve you better.

Enjoy exploring Cortana's capabilities as part of your journey with Windows 11, and most importantly, have fun along the way! As you become more accustomed to asking for assistance and accessing information through your voice, you'll discover the significant benefits of incorporating modern technology into your everyday activities.

ACCESSIBILITY FEATURES FOR EASIER USE

Navigating through new technology can be daunting, especially when dealing with a variety of accessibility needs that may come with age. Fortunately, Windows 11 is designed with numerous built-in accessibility features that cater specifically to enhancing usability for all users, including seniors. These features aim to make your computer easier to see, hear, and use, thus greatly enhancing your computing experience.

Exploring Windows 11 Accessibility Features

Windows 11 has been designed with inclusivity in mind, ensuring that everyone, regardless of their physical abilities, can use their PC independently and comfortably. Here's a detailed look at some of the key accessibility features:

Vision Accessibility

- **Narrator**: A built-in screen reader that reads text on the screen aloud and describes events, notifications, or actions that happen while you're using your PC. It's particularly helpful for those with severe visual impairments.
    - **Turning It On**: Go to Settings → Accessibility → Narrator and switch on the Narrator toggle.
- **Magnifier**: This tool zooms in part or all of your screen making text, images, and objects easier to see.
    - **Activating Magnifier**: Press the Windows logo key + Plus (+) to turn it on.
- **High Contrast Themes**: These themes change the color and contrast of your desktop and applications to make content easier to read.
    - **Setting Up**: Navigate to Settings → Accessibility → Contrast themes, and pick a theme that works best for you.
- **Text Size and Brightness**: Adjusting the text size and screen brightness can make the screen more comfortable to view.
    - **Adjusting Settings**: Settings → Accessibility → Text size, where you can slide to adjust the font size as needed.

Hearing Accessibility

- **Closed Captions**: Customize captions for videos to make sure they are easy to read.
    - **Customization**: Go to Settings → Accessibility → Captions, and choose the preferences for color, size, and transparency.
- **Visual Notifications**: Instead of sounds, you can set up visual cues for system alerts.
    - **Enabling This Feature**: Settings → Accessibility → Audio, and toggle on visual notifications.

Mobility Accessibility

- **Sticky Keys**: For people who have difficulty pressing shortcuts that require multiple keys at once, sticky keys let you press them sequentially.
    - **Enable Sticky Keys**: Press the Shift key five times rapidity or go to Settings → Accessibility → Keyboard and turn on Sticky Keys.
- **On-Screen Keyboard**: Allows you to type using a mouse or another pointing device by tapping keys on a virtual keyboard displayed on the screen.
    - **Accessing the Keyboard**: Settings → Accessibility → Keyboard, and switch on the On-Screen Keyboard.
- **Speech Recognition**: Operate your PC using voice commands, from launching applications to dictating and editing text.

- ○ **Activating Speech Recognition**: Navigate to Settings → Accessibility → Speech, and turn on Windows Speech Recognition.

Cognitive Accessibility

- **Focus Assist**: Helps minimize distractions by filtering notifications when you need to stay focused.
  - ○ **Configuration**: Settings → System → Focus assist and select from Priority Only or Alarms Only options.
- **Reading and Writing Tools**: Technologies like Microsoft's "Read Aloud" in Edge or Word can read texts aloud, helping those with dyslexia or other learning differences.
  - ○ **Using Read Aloud**: In Microsoft Edge, right-click a webpage and select "Read aloud."

Customizing Your Accessibility Preferences

For ease of access, you can customize these settings to create your optimal setup:

1. **Quick Access to Settings**:
   - ○ Use Windows logo key + U to open Accessibility settings quickly.
2. **Accessibility Shortcut**:
   - ○ Press the Windows logo key + Ctrl + M to open the accessibility settings menu from any screen.
3. **Save Your Preferences**:
   - ○ Once you have adjusted the settings to meet your needs, Windows 11 allows you to save these preferences associated with your user account.

Conclusion

Embracing these accessibility features in Windows 11 not only maximizes your comfort but also ensures your computing experience is both enjoyable and efficient. By tailoring each feature to meet your specific needs, you can enhance your ability to stay connected, productive, and entertained. Remember, technology is here to make your life easier, and Windows 11 is equipped to help you achieve just that.

EXPLORING WINDOWS SETTINGS FOR PERSONAL CONVENIENCE

Navigating the Windows Settings might seem like a trek through unfamiliar territory at first glance, but with a bit of guidance and some helpful tips, you'll find it's designed to enhance your daily computer use significantly. This part of your journey with Windows 11 is about personalization and setting up your PC in a way that fits perfectly with your lifestyle and needs. Let's walk through the key aspects of Windows Settings that you should be aware of, ensuring your experience is tailored just for you.

Accessing Windows Settings

First things first, let's explore how to open the Windows Settings: - **Step 1**: Click on the Start button (the Windows icon in the bottom-left corner of your screen).

- **Step 2**: Click on the gear-shaped icon labeled 'Settings'. Alternatively, you can press the Windows logo key + I on your keyboard to open Settings directly.

Personalizing Your Experience

Once you're in the Settings menu, you will see several options listed on the left, each leading to different customization and configuration possibilities. Here are some key areas you might find useful:

System Settings

- **Display**: Adjust the brightness and scale of your display to ensure text, apps, and other items are easy to see. Simply go to System → Display.

- **Sound**: Here, you can adjust the volume, choose your input and output devices, and manage other sound settings to better suit your hearing preferences. This is found under System → Sound.
- **Notifications & actions**: You can customize how you receive alerts and which apps can send you notifications. Control the chaos and keep only the essential notifications active.

Network & Internet

- **Wi-Fi**: Connect to new networks or manage existing connections. Go to Network & Internet → Wi-Fi.
- **Data Usage**: Monitor how much data you're using if you have a limited data plan. This helps prevent any unexpected charges.

Personalization

- **Background**: Change the desktop background with an image you love, a slideshow, or a solid color to make your workspace more you. Find this under Personalization → Background.
- **Colors**: Choose a color theme that's easy on your eyes. You can set it to be light, dark, or custom.
- **Lock Screen**: Customize your lock screen with preferred images and select which apps show quick status. This setting can be adjusted in Personalization → Lock Screen.

Accounts

- **Your Info**: Check and manage your account details and profile picture. Adjust settings related to sign-in options and access work or school accounts under Accounts.

Time & Language

- **Date & Time**: Ensure your computer's clock is always right, which is crucial for appointments and reminders. Navigate through Time & Language → Date & Time.
- **Language**: Add and shift between different languages for your display and keyboard layout.

Ease of Access

This is the dedicated section for accessibility settings, catering to needs ranging from vision and hearing enhancements to interaction adaptations:

- **Visual Aids**: These options include text size adjustments, magnifiers, or high contrast themes.
- **Audio Options**: Features like audio alerts visual notifications ensure you don't miss important cues if you have a hard time hearing sounds from your computer.
- **Interaction**: Adjust settings for the keyboard, mouse, speech recognition, and more to make interacting with your device easier.

Using Search in Settings

If you're looking for a specific setting or need help with a particular feature, use the search bar at the top of the Settings window. Type keywords related to what you're adjusting, and it will guide you to the right option.

Keeping Your System Updated

Lastly, keeping your PC updated: - **Check for Updates**: Go to Update & Security → Windows Update, and then click on 'Check for updates'. Keeping your OS updated ensures you have the latest features and security improvements.

Conclusion

The Windows Settings on your Windows 11 machine are your gateway to making the PC experience your own. Spend time getting to know these settings, experimenting with what they do, and adjusting them to suit your needs. With this understanding, you have the power to shape how you interact with your technology, making every day a little easier and a lot more enjoyable. Always remember, your computer should work for you, not the other way around!

13. STAYING CONNECTED WITH SOCIAL MEDIA

SETTING UP A FACEBOOK ACCOUNT

In today's digital age, staying connected with family and friends is more important than ever. One of the most popular platforms for this is Facebook. Setting up a Facebook account allows you to share photos, join groups, engage in conversations, and much more. Let's walk through the process of creating your Facebook profile, ensuring you can navigate this social platform safely and confidently.

Why Facebook?

Facebook can serve as a wonderful bridge connecting you to the lives of loved ones near and far. Whether it's seeing pictures of your grandchildren, reconnecting with old friends, or joining groups that match your interests, Facebook shapes these connections into an easy-to-navigate social landscape.

Step-by-Step Guide to Setting Up Your Facebook Account

1. **Access the Facebook Website**
    o   Open your preferred web browser.
    o   Type www.facebook.com in the address bar.
    o   Press Enter on your keyboard, and the Facebook homepage will load.

2. **Sign Up for a New Account**
    o   On the Facebook homepage, you will see a section titled Sign Up.
    o   Fill in your first and last name.
    o   Enter your mobile number or email address. This will be used to verify your account.
    o   Choose a password for your account. Make it strong by using a combination of letters, numbers, and symbols.
    o   Select your birthdate from the drop-down menus.
    o   Choose your gender by clicking on the appropriate option.
    o   Once all fields are filled, click on the green Sign Up button to continue.

3. **Verify Your Account**
    o   Facebook will send a verification code to your email or phone. Check your messages to find this code.
    o   Enter the verification code in the space provided on the website.
    o   Click Continue to verify your account.

4. **Set Up Your Profile**
    o   After verification, you'll be prompted to set up your profile.
    o   Add a profile picture by clicking on Add Picture. Choose a photo that makes it easy for others to recognize you, such as a clear headshot.

- You may also add your current city, education, and places you've worked. This information is optional but helps friends find you on the platform.

5. **Find Friends**
   - Facebook can help you find people you may know by using your email contacts.
   - You can opt to provide permission to search your email contacts or skip this step.
   - Alternatively, you can search for specific people using the search bar at the top.

6. **Adjust Your Privacy Settings**
   - Click on the downward triangle at the top right of the Facebook page and select Settings & Privacy, then Settings.
   - Click on Privacy in the left-hand menu.
   - Review the options and customize who can see your posts, send you friend requests, and how people can look you up. Setting these to 'Friends' is often a good starting point for privacy.

7. **Understanding the News Feed and Posting**
   - The central part of your Facebook screen is known as the News Feed. Here you will see updates from your friends and any groups or pages you follow.
   - To create a post, click on the box at the top of the News Feed where it says What's on your mind, [Your Name]?
   - You can type a message, share photos or videos, or post links to other websites.

8. **Join Groups and Like Pages**
   - Explore your interests by joining groups or liking pages.
   - Use the search bar to find groups related to hobbies or topics you enjoy.
   - To join a group, click on the group name, then click Join Group.
   - To like a page, just click the Like button near the page name.

9. **Engaging Safely**
   - When sharing information or photos, always consider who can see what you post. Adjust your post visibility if necessary.
   - Be wary of friend requests from people you do not know as they might be fake profiles.
   - Never share sensitive personal information like your home address, phone number, or banking details.

Reconnecting and Enjoying Connections

Now that your account is set up, take some time to explore Facebook. Reconnect with friends, discover community events, or find support in one of the many groups tailored to various interests and needs. Remember, it's your digital space, so manage it in a way that brings joy and adds value to your everyday life.

With these steps, you should feel more confident in managing your new Facebook account. Engage at your pace and explore the features that interest you the most. Social media is a powerful tool for staying connected, and now you're well-prepared to use it effectively and securely. Happy connecting!

SHARING PHOTOS AND VIDEOS ONLINE

Sharing precious moments through photos and videos is one of the most enjoyable ways to keep in touch with family and friends online. Whether it's snapshots from a recent trip, a video of a family gathering, or just everyday moments, embracing technology to share these memories can be rewarding and fun. Let's explore how you can share photos and videos on popular social media platforms with ease and confidence.

Selecting Your Platform

Several platforms are favorites for sharing photos and videos:

- **Facebook**: Great for sharing with a specific group of family or friends and engaging through likes and comments.
- **Instagram**: Perfect for photo and short video sharing, with options to use visual enhancements like filters.

- **Pinterest**: Ideal for creating collections of images that inspire you or others, often used for hobbies or interest projects.

Preparing to Share Photos and Videos

Before you upload or share any content, here are some key steps to prepare:

1. **Choose Your Content**: Select the photos or videos you want to share from your device. Consider their clarity and ensure they depict exactly what you want to show your friends and family.
2. **Organize Your Files**: If you're planning to upload multiple files, organize them in folders on your computer or device. This makes it easier to locate and choose them when you start the uploading process.
3. **Edit as Needed**: You might want to crop photos for better framing or adjust brightness and contrast. Tools like Windows Photo Viewer or Photos App on Windows 11 offer basic editing options.
4. **Check File Sizes**: Some platforms have limits on the file size or type you can upload. Videos, especially, may need to be under a certain duration or file size. Check the platform's guidelines before uploading.

Uploading Photos and Videos to Social Media

Using Facebook

1. **Log in to Your Account**: Open your browser, go to www.facebook.com, and log in with your credentials.
2. **Access the Photo/Video Upload function**:
   - On your homepage, click on 'Photo/Video' in the 'Create Post' box at the top.
   - Choose whether to post on your profile or share in a specific group.
3. **Upload Your Files**:
   - Click 'Upload Photos/Videos'.
   - Select the files from your designated folder. You can select multiple files by holding Ctrl and clicking each one.

o Add comments or tags to your photos if you like, tagging friends or locations can be done by typing the '@' symbol followed by the name.

4. **Share Your Post**:

    o Once ready, click 'Post'. Your photos and videos will then be shared with your chosen audience, based on your privacy settings.

Using Instagram

1. **Open the App**: On your smartphone or tablet, open the Instagram app. Log in if not already signed in.

2. **Add a Photo or Video**:

    o Tap the '+' icon at the bottom of the screen.

    o Choose 'Post'. You can now take a new photo/video or pick one from your gallery.

    o After selecting, click 'Next'. You can now apply filters or edit.

3. **Share Your Content**:

    o After editing, press 'Next'.

    o Add a caption and decide if you want to share it on other social networks connected to your Instagram.

    o Hit 'Share' at the top right corner.

Using Pinterest

1. **Access Your Account**: Open Pinterest on your browser or through the app and log into your account.

2. **Create a New Pin**:

    o Click on your profile, then 'Create Pin'.

    o Drag and drop or upload an image from your computer.

    o Add a title, a description, and the URL of the website it's from (if applicable).

3. **Choose a Board**:

    o Select or create a board to pin to.

    o Once all information is complete, click 'Save'.

Best Practices for Online Safety

When sharing online:

- **Adjust Privacy Settings**: Always check who can view your photos and videos. Adjust settings to either public, friends only, or private as necessary.

– **Think Before You Post**: Reflect on whether the content is something you're comfortable with everyone potentially seeing.

- **Secure Your Accounts**: Use strong, unique passwords for all social media to prevent unauthorized access. Enable two-factor authentication for added security.

Enjoy the Process

Take pleasure in sharing the highlights of your life. Engaging with others online over shared memories can bring joy and a sense of closeness, even if miles apart. Don't rush—take your time to enjoy the process, explore different platforms, and see which ones best suit your desire to stay connected. Happy sharing!

CONNECTING WITH INTEREST GROUPS AND PAGES

Social media opens doors to vast communities and networks that align with your personal passions, hobbies, and interests. Whether you are keen on gardening, love book clubs, or are an avid fan of classic cars, social media platforms can connect you with groups and pages filled with like-minded individuals. This segment will guide you through finding these communities, joining them, and interacting within them safely and enjoyably.

Understanding Groups and Pages

Groups are usually gatherings of individuals who share a common interest. They can be open for anyone to join, or they can be private, requiring approval.

Pages are typically created by businesses, public figures, or for promotional purposes. They are public, and you can follow these to receive updates without necessarily engaging directly.

Finding and Joining Interest Groups on Facebook

1. **Log Into Facebook**
   - Begin by opening your web browser, going to www.facebook.com, and logging into your account.

2. **Use the Search Feature**
   - At the top of your Facebook page, you'll see a search bar. Type in a keyword related to your interest. For example, if you're interested in photography, type "photography groups."

3. **Exploring the Results**
   - Your search results will include a mix of posts, pages, groups, and more. Click on the 'Groups' tab to filter the results to only include groups.

4. **Choosing a Group**
   - Scan through the list of groups. Look at the number of members and read the description to see if it matches your interests.
   - Check if the group is public or private. Public groups let you see the content and join immediately. Private groups require you to request membership and await approval.

5. **Joining Groups**
   - For public groups, simply click 'Join Group'. For private groups, click 'Join Group' and possibly answer questions set by administrators, which helps them understand why you're interested in joining.

6. **Engage with Content**
   - Once part of a group, start engaging by liking posts, commenting, or even sharing relevant content. Make sure to observe group rules and etiquette, maintaining courteous and respectful interactions.

Following Interest Pages on Facebook

1. **Find Pages**
   - Use the search bar at the top of your Facebook homepage to type in your interest. For example, you might type "vintage cars." After typing your interest, select the 'Pages' tab.

2. **Selecting a Page**
   - Check out different pages by going to their profile. See what kind of content they share, how often they post, and the number of followers they have.

3. **Following Pages**
   - If you find a page that interests you, click the 'Like' or 'Follow' button. This action will ensure updates from the page appear on your news feed.

Engaging in Online Communities

- **Stay Active**: Regularly participate in discussions, polls, and other activities within the group or page. Active participation increases your visibility and connection with the community.
- **Share Wisely**: Share relevant articles, videos, and thoughts that add value to the discussion. Avoid oversharing personal information.
- **Use Alerts**: Set up notifications for your favorite groups and pages, so you don't miss out on new content or discussions.

Safety and Privacy Online

- **Review Privacy Settings**: Regularly check your privacy settings to control who can see what you post in groups and on pages.
- **Be Cautious**: Be mindful of scams or misleading information. Verify information before sharing it.
- **Respect Differences**: Social media is a global platform. People from different backgrounds and beliefs may express differing opinions. Always approach disagreements with respect.

Making the Most of Your Experience

Connecting with online communities is not just about sharing and receiving information; it's also about building relationships and learning from others. As you become more comfortable navigating these digital spaces, you'll find that they significantly enhance your daily life by allowing you to explore your interests in new and exciting ways.*SHAREDENTHUSIASMEnd the sub-chapter with encouraging seniors to take the leap into joining online communities, highlighting the joy and enrichment it can bring into their lives.RELATABLECALLTOACTION*

14. PHOTOS AND MULTIMEDIA

ORGANIZING AND VIEWING PHOTOS

Organizing and viewing photos on your computer can bring immense joy, especially when those pictures are of cherished memories, family gatherings, and important life events. With Windows 11, managing these precious snapshots is straightforward, ensuring that even if you're new to technology, you can easily keep your photos organized and accessible. Let's walk through the process step by step.

Step 1: Opening Your Photos App

First, let's locate and open the Photos app on your Windows 11 computer:

1. Click on the **Start menu** at the bottom-left corner of your screen.
2. Type "Photos" into the search bar.
3. Click on the **Photos app** icon that appears in the search results.

This app serves as your go-to hub for all photo-related activities, including viewing, organizing, and editing.

Step 2: Importing Photos to Your Computer

If your photos are not yet on your computer, here's how to add them:

From a Camera or Phone:

1. Connect your device (camera or smartphone) to the computer using a USB cable.
2. A notification might pop up asking what you'd like to do with the device. Choose **Import Photos and Videos**.
3. Follow the on-screen instructions to select which photos to import.

From a CD or External Storage:

1. Insert the CD into your computer's drive or connect the external storage device.
2. Open the folder containing the photos.
3. Select the photos you want to import, then right-click and choose **Copy**.
4. Navigate to the Pictures folder on your computer, right-click and select **Paste**.

Transferring photos onto your computer is the first essential step in organizing your digital memories.

Step 3: Viewing Photos in the App

Once your photos are on the computer, view them in the Photos app:

1. Open the Photos app if it's not already open.
2. Click on **Collection** from the left-hand menu to see all your photos and videos.
3. Click on any photo to open it in full view.

Step 4: Creating Albums

Creating albums organizes your photos into meaningful groups:

1. In the Photos app, click **Albums** on the left menu, then click **New album**.
2. Select the photos you would like to add to the album.
3. Click the **Add** button at the top right.
4. Name your album accordingly and then press **Enter**.

Albums can be practical, like "Family Reunions 2023," or themed by season or location.

Step 5: Searching for Photos

Finding a specific photo is easy with the search functionality in the Photos app:

1. In the Photos app, click the **Search** icon in the top right corner.

2. You can type in dates, places, or even things (like "beach" or "dog") and the app will use its intelligent search to find relevant photos.

Step 6: Editing Photos

To enhance or make small corrections to your photos:

1. Open the photo you wish to edit by double-clicking on it.
2. Click on **Edit & Create** on the toolbar.
3. Choose from options like **Edit**, **Draw**, or **Add 3D effects**.
4. Make your changes and click **Save**. Always save a copy to preserve the original photo.

Step 7: Backing Up Your Photos

Ensuring your photos are backed up is crucial in case of computer issues:

1. Consider using **OneDrive**, Microsoft's online storage service. Windows 11 integrates seamlessly with OneDrive.
2. Sign in or create a OneDrive account, then upload your Photos folder by dragging it into the OneDrive folder in your File Explorer.

Step 8: Sharing Photos

Share your pictures with friends or colleagues directly from the Photos app:

1. Select the photo(s) you want to share.
2. Click the **Share** icon at the top right of the app window.
3. Choose how you want to share: via email, nearby sharing, or posting directly to social media platforms.

Additional Tips

- Regularly update your photo albums to keep them organized.
- Use facial recognition features in the app to quickly find pictures of specific people.
- Make use of tags or favorites to mark photos you access frequently.

By following these straightforward steps, managing your photographic memories on Windows 11 becomes an enjoyable activity rather than a daunting task. Windows 11 is designed to make photo organization accessible and fun, allowing you to focus on reliving the good times and sharing those moments with others.

BASIC PHOTO EDITING TECHNIQUES

Editing photos might seem like a task reserved for professionals, but Windows 11 has made it surprisingly simple for everyone, including seniors who might be taking their first steps in digital photo enhancement. Let's explore basic photo editing techniques using the built-in Photos app, enabling you to polish your snapshots into treasured keepsakes.

Opening Your Photo for Editing

Before you start editing, you need to open your photo in the Photos app:

1. Click on the **Start menu** at the bottom-left of your screen.
2. Type "Photos" into the search bar and open the **Photos app**.
3. Navigate to the photo you wish to edit and click on it to open.

Basic Editing Tools

Once your photo is open, enter the editing mode:

1. Click the **Edit & Create** button at the top of the window.
2. Select **Edit** from the dropdown menu to access the editing tools.

Here are some basic tools and how to use them:

1. Crop and Rotate

- **Cropping** helps you frame the photo to focus on the desired subject and improve the composition. Click on **Crop**, and you'll see handles appear around your photo. Drag these handles to adjust the frame.
- **Rotation** is useful if your photo is not straight. Use the rotation button to turn your photo left or right.

2. Adjustment Sliders

Adjustment sliders control the brightness, contrast, and color of your photo:

- **Brightness**: Makes your photo lighter or darker.

- **Contrast**: Enhances the differences between light and dark areas.

- **Saturation**: Increases or reduces color intensity.

Drag each slider left or right to make adjustments until you're happy with how your photo looks.

3. Filters

Filters are pre-set adjustments that change the look of your photo with a single click. Here's how to apply a filter:

- Click **Filters** on the editing menu.

- Browse through the available options and click on one to apply it to your photo.

Enhancing and Fine-Tuning

After making basic adjustments, you might want to fine-tune your photo:

Red-eye Removal

If your photo has a subject with 'red eyes' from flash photography, you can fix this:

- Click **Edit and Create**, then choose **Edit**.

- Use the **Red-eye removal** tool by clicking on each red eye in the photo.

Spot Fix

Sometimes, photos have unwanted spots or blemishes:

- Select the **Spot fix** tool from the Edit menu.

- Click on the spots you wish to remove. Windows 11 will automatically blend them into the background.

Saving Your Edited Photo

Once you are satisfied with your edits, it's time to save your work:

1. Click **Save** or **Save a copy** to keep the original photo unchanged.
2. Choose where to save your photo and enter a file name.

Sharing Your Edited Photo

Now that your photo looks great, you might want to share it:

- Click the **Share** icon at the top of the Photos app.

- Choose how to share (e.g., email, social media).

Advanced Options for Creativity

Windows 11 also offers some advanced editing features for when you're feeling creative:

Adding Text

You can add text to personalize your photos:

- Click **Edit & Create**, then **Add text**.

- Type your message and place it wherever you like on the photo.

Drawing

If you want to draw on your photo:

- Choose **Draw** from the Edit & Create menu.

- Select a pen, pencil, or highlighter from the drawing tools and use your mouse (or your finger, if you have a touchscreen) to draw on your photo.

3D Effects

For a bit of fun, you can add 3D effects:

- Select **3D effects** from the Edit menu.

- Choose an effect and adjust its placement and orientation in your photo.

Using these simple yet effective tools, you can enhance your family photos, vacation snaps, or any other pictures, turning them from simple images into stories worth sharing. Being able to edit your photos is not just about adjusting how they look; it's about bringing out the emotions and memories they capture. Remember, the joy of photo editing lies in experimentation and personal expression. So, take your time, try different tools, and most importantly, have fun as you make your photos truly your own.

LISTENING TO MUSIC AND PODCASTS

In the digital age, enjoying music and podcasts has never been easier, and with Windows 11, seniors can easily access a vast world of auditory entertainment. Whether it's classical music, the latest pop hits, or engaging podcasts covering news, hobbies, or stories, everything you need is right at your fingertips. Let's dive into how you can start listening to your favorite music and podcasts directly from your Windows 11 device.

Getting Started with Music and Podcasts on Windows 11

To begin, you'll need to know where and how you can access music and podcasts. There are several straightforward options available:

Using Built-in Apps

Windows 11 comes with pre-installed apps that can play music and podcasts you already own or have downloaded:

1. **Groove Music**: Primarily used for music, Groove Music is a user-friendly app where you can play and organize your music files.

2. **Windows Media Player**: A classic choice that supports both music and video playback. It's perfect for those who prefer a familiar interface.

How to Open Groove Music:

- Click on the **Start menu**.
- Scroll through the list of apps or type "Groove Music" in the search bar.
- Click on the app to open it.

How to Play Music in Groove Music:

- Once open, you can add your music files to Groove Music by dragging them into the window or by clicking **File** then **Open** to select music files from your folders.
- Your music will appear in your playlist. Click any song to start playing it. You can also create custom playlists.

Streaming Music and Podcasts

Streaming services offer vast libraries of music and podcasts that you can access anytime, as long as you have an internet connection. Here are a few popular services:

- **Spotify**: Offers both free and premium accounts for streaming music and podcasts.

- **Apple Music**: A subscription service known for its extensive music collection.
- **Audible**: While primarily known for audiobooks, it also offers podcast streaming.

How to Access These Services:

- Open your web browser from the **Start menu** or desktop.
- Type the website address for the service (e.g., spotify.com) in the URL bar.
- Follow the instructions on the site to sign up or log in.

How to Install Apps for Streaming Services:

- Click on the **Microsoft Store** icon on your taskbar or search for it in the Start menu.
- In the Microsoft Store, search for the app (e.g., "Spotify").
- Click **Get** or **Install** to download and install the app.

Listening to a Podcast

Podcasts are like radio shows you can subscribe to and listen to at your leisure. They cover a broad range of topics, and you can find them on streaming services like Spotify or dedicated podcast apps like Google Podcasts or Apple Podcasts.

How to Start Listening to Podcasts:

- Install a podcast app from the Microsoft Store as described above.
- Open the app and use the search feature to find a podcast by topic or name.
- Subscribe to the podcast to keep updated with new episodes.

Managing Volume and Sound Settings

When listening to music or podcasts, managing the sound settings ensures a comfortable listening experience:

1. **Adjust Volume**: Click on the speaker icon in the lower-right corner of your taskbar to adjust the volume slider.
2. **Sound Settings**: Right-click the speaker icon and select **Open Sound settings** to customize output devices (like headphones or speakers) and sound quality.

Organizing Your Music and Podcasts

Keeping your media organized will help you easily locate your favorite music and podcasts:

- **Create Playlists**: In apps like Groove Music and Spotify, you can create playlists to organize songs by mood, genre, or any other preference.
- **Bookmarking Favorite Podcasts**: Most podcast apps allow you to mark favorite shows or episodes, making them easier to find later.

Benefits of Engaging with Music and Podcasts

Besides entertainment, regularly listening to music and podcasts can have profound benefits: - **Cognitive Stimulation**: Music and conversational podcasts can keep the mind engaged and sharp. - **Emotional Wellbeing**: Music has been shown to reduce stress and elevate mood. - **Staying Informed and Connected**: Podcasts can be a source of news and can connect you with communities of like-minded listeners.

By following these steps, you can begin enjoying music and podcasts on your Windows 11 device. Whether it's through downloading and playing your files on Groove Music, streaming on Spotify, or following interesting podcasts, there's an abundance of auditory content waiting for you to explore and enjoy. Embrace this digital convenience to enhance your daily routines, connect with your passions, and possibly discover new ones.

WATCHING MOVIES AND STREAMING VIDEO

In the digital era, enjoying your favorite movies and videos from the comfort of your home is a simple pleasure that Windows 11 enhances wonderfully. This guide will explore how you can utilize your new operating system to watch movies and stream videos effectively and comfortably. Let's embark on your journey into the world of digital storytelling and video content.

Preparing to Watch Movies and Videos

Before diving into watching a movie or video, ensure your device is properly set up for an enjoyable viewing experience:

Choosing a Default Media Player

Windows 11 comes with built-in media players, but you can choose the one that suits your preferences best, such as VLC or Windows Media Player.

To set a default media player:

1. Click **Start** and then **Settings**.
2. Navigate to **Apps** and then to **Default apps**.
3. Scroll to find the file type (like .mp4 for videos) and choose the app you want to use as the default.

Adjusting Display Settings

For a better viewing experience, adjust your screen's display settings, especially if you watch on a laptop or an attached monitor.

To adjust display settings:

1. Right-click on your desktop and select **Display settings**.
2. Adjust the **Scale and layout** to enhance text and image visibility.
3. Modify the **Resolution** for optimal clarity according to your monitor specifications.

Using Streaming Services on Windows 11

Streaming services like Netflix, Amazon Prime Video, or YouTube offer vast libraries of movies, TV shows, and other video content available at a click:

Accessing Streaming Services

You can access these services either through their respective websites in a web browser or via apps installed from the Microsoft Store.

To install a streaming service app:

1. Open **Microsoft Store** from the taskbar or Start menu.
2. Use the search bar at the top-right corner and type in the name of the service (e.g., "Netflix").
3. Select the app and click **Install**.

Signing in or creating an account:

1. Once installed, open the app.
2. Follow the prompts to sign in or create a new account.
3. Choose the subscription plan if required and provide payment details.

Navigating Streaming Services

Most streaming platforms have similar layouts, where you can browse categories, search for specific titles, or view curated lists such as "Recommended for You."

Basic navigation tips:

- Use the **Search** bar to find specific shows or movies.

- Check out different **Categories or Genres** to explore available content.

Downloading Movies and Videos for Offline Viewing

Many streaming services allow you to download movies and shows on your device, which is perfect for watching without an internet connection:

To download content:

1. Select the movie or show you want to watch.
2. Look for a **Download** icon (usually an arrow pointing downward) and click it.
3. Wait for the download to complete, then access it anytime from the app's library under "Downloads" or a similar section.

Watching DVDs and Blu-ray Discs

If you own physical copies of movies or TV shows, you can watch them by using a DVD or Blu-ray drive in your computer.

To watch a DVD or Blu-ray:

1. Insert the disc into the DVD or Blu-ray drive.
2. Open your preferred media player. It might auto-play. If not, open the player and select the disc from the listed options.
3. Controls for play, pause, and navigation will appear in the media player interface.

Adjusting Audio Settings for Optimal Sound

Ensuring the audio settings are optimized can make a world of difference:

To adjust audio settings:

1. Right-click the **speaker icon** on your taskbar.
2. Select **Open Sound settings**.
3. Under **Output**, choose your sound output device, and adjust the volume slider as needed.

Utilizing Accessibility Features for Enhanced Viewing

Windows 11 includes features to help everyone enjoy movies and videos:

Key accessibility features:

- **Subtitles and closed captions**: Can be enabled in most media players and streaming apps. Look for a CC button or similar in the settings.
- **Audio descriptions**: Provide narration for what's happening on-screen, helpful for those with visual impairments.

By following these steps, watching movies and streaming videos on Windows 11 should be a breeze even if you're new to using this operating system. From adjusting settings for optimum viewing pleasure to downloading favorite shows for offline enjoyment, Windows 11 facilitates a comprehensive and enjoyable multimedia experience. So, grab some popcorn, settle in, and immerse yourself in the video content of your choice with just a few clicks.

15. GETTING HELP AND SUPPORT
USING WINDOWS 11 HELP AND TIPS

Navigating new technology can sometimes feel like learning a new language, especially with the constant updates and innovations. However, Windows 11 comes equipped with several helpful resources designed to ease this learning curve. **Windows 11 Help and Tips** is a built-in feature that serves as your personal guide and troubleshooter, ensuring you're never left in the dark as you explore your new operating system. Here's how you can make the most out of these resources, turning potential frustrations into learning opportunities.

Accessing Windows 11 Help and Tips

To start using Windows 11 Help and Tips, you don't need to go far. It's easily accessible and can provide instant answers and guidance.

- **Open Start Menu**: Click the Start button (the Windows icon in the bottom-left corner of your screen).
- **Search for Help**: In the search bar, type Help and Support. This will bring up the Help and Tips application.
- **Launch the Application**: Click on the application from the search results to open it. You will be greeted with a variety of topics tailored to help new users find their way around Windows 11.

Using the Search Function in Help and Tips

If you have a specific question or need information on a particular feature, the search function within the Help and Tips app is incredibly useful.

- **Enter Your Query**: Simply type a keyword or question into the search bar. For example, type "how to connect to Wi-Fi" or "change desktop background".
- **Browse the Results**: You will see a list of help articles and step-by-step guides that pertain to your query. Click on any of the results to read more detailed information.

Exploring Topics on Common Features

Windows 11 Help and Tips is organized into several sections, each focusing on different aspects of the operating system.

- **Start Menu**: Learn how to customize and use the Start Menu to access apps, settings, and files faster.
- **System Settings**: Adjust your system settings for better personalization and functionality.
- **Security**: Understand how to protect your computer from viruses and malware and how to set up Windows Defender.

Interactive Guides and Tutorials

One of the most useful features in the Help and Tips app are the interactive guides and video tutorials. These are designed for those who learn best through visual aids and step-by-step walkthroughs.

- **Follow Along**: Start an interactive guide. It will direct you to perform actions while providing on-screen instructions.
- **Watch Videos**: If you prefer watching to reading, there are short videos that explain how to use different features of Windows 11.

Staying Updated with Tips

Every once in a while, Windows 11 gets updates that may add new features or change existing ones. The Tips section helps you stay updated.

- **Check Regularly**: Return to the Tips section periodically to see what's new or might have changed.
- **Practice**: Try out the tips to get a hands-on experience with new features.

Feedback and Support

Your feedback is crucial for improving future versions of Windows.

- **Give Feedback**: In the Help and Tips app, you'll find options to send feedback to Microsoft. This could be about a particularly helpful article or something you think could be improved.

Bookmarking Useful Guides

As you explore and learn, you might find particular guides or tips more useful than others.

- **Add to Favorites**: Most web browsers and Help sections allow you to bookmark or save these resources, so you can easily return to them without a new search.

Printing Out Guides

For those who prefer hard copies over digital ones:

- **Print Option**: Look for a print icon or option within the Help and Tips application. This way, you can have a physical copy of the most useful guides that you can refer to anytime, without needing your computer on.

Summary

Windows 11 Help and Tips is a comprehensive tool designed to help you understand and navigate your new operating system with ease. By exploring its different features, from searchable help articles to interactive tutorials, it provides a robust support system right at your fingertips. Remember, learning new technology takes time and patience, but with these resources, you are never alone on this journey. Always keep exploring and practicing, and soon, you'll find yourself more confident and capable in managing and enjoying your Windows 11 experience.

ONLINE COMMUNITIES AND FORUMS

When you step into the world of Windows 11, remember that you're not alone. Many others are also learning and exploring, just like you. Online communities and forums offer a wealth of information and a space to share experiences, solutions, and receive support. Let's discover how you can engage with these resources to enhance your journey with Windows 11.

Discover and Engage with Online Communities and Forums

Online communities and forums are platforms where users can post questions, share information, or discuss specific topics. They can be particularly useful when you're looking for fast answers or insights from other experienced users.

1. Identifying Relevant Communities

- **Microsoft Community**: Start with the official Microsoft Community page. It's a rich resource for discussions specifically related to Microsoft products, including Windows 11.
- **Reddit**: Look for subreddits like r/Windows or r/Windows11 where users frequently discuss features, updates, and troubleshooting tips regarding Windows operating systems.
- **Tech Support Forums**: Websites like Tech Support Guy or Bleeping Computer are useful for getting help with more technical issues.

2. Signing Up and Participating

- **Create an Account**: Usually, you'll need to make an account to participate in forums. This typically involves setting up a username and password.
- **Search for Topics**: Use the search function within the forum to find discussions related to your questions or interests.
- **Ask Questions**: Don't hesitate to post your own questions. Remember to be as specific as possible to increase the chances of receiving helpful answers.

- **Answer Questions**: If you see a question and you know the answer, feel free to contribute. Sharing knowledge is what keeps these communities thriving.

3. Navigating Forums Safely

- **Stay Private**: Be cautious with your personal information. Avoid sharing anything too specific about your identity or location.
- **Verify Responses**: While forums are great for advice, ensure to verify the solutions from a couple of different sources especially if it involves changing system settings.
- **Be Respectful**: Respect others' opinions and remember that everyone was a beginner at one point. Encourage and support fellow users.

Benefits of Engaging with Online Communities

Online communities can be more than just problem-solving resources; they are virtual spaces to connect with like-minded individuals.

- **Learning New Tips and Tricks**: Regular participation can expose you to tips and tricks that you might not find in manuals or official guides.
- **Staying Updated**: Members of tech forums often share the latest news about updates and features, which can help you stay current with your software.
- **Social Interaction**: For many, these forums also provide a sense of community and interaction which can be particularly rewarding.

Tips for Effective Forum Use

Here are some tips to make your time on tech forums more effective:

- **Bookmark Useful Threads**: If you find a discussion or a tutorial helpful, bookmark it on your web browser for easy access in the future.
- **Utilize Forum Tools**: Use tools provided by the forum like 'thread subscription' or 'post notifications' to keep track of discussions you're involved in.
- **Be Patient**: Sometimes it might take a while before someone responds to your query. Be patient or try to rephrase and repost your question if you don't receive an answer.

Problem-Solving with Community Insights

Often, the solutions offered in online forums are born from real-life experience and tested by ordinary users. This practical advice can sometimes be more tailored and effective than official troubleshooting steps.

- **Follow Step-by-Step Guides**: Many forum users post detailed instructions or tutorials that can be easier to follow than standard help docs.
- **Look for Pinned Posts**: Most forums pin the most important or useful posts at the top for easy access. These often include FAQs or common troubleshooting steps.

Conclusion

As you navigate Windows 11, consider online communities and forums as your companions in the journey. They are a testament to the collaborative spirit of the internet, filled with individuals eager to assist and learn from one another. By joining these communities, not only do you gain access to a vast amount of information and support, but you also contribute to a shared pool of knowledge that can help others. Dive in with an open mind and a bit of caution, and you'll find that help is always just a post away.

CONTACTING MICROSOFT SUPPORT

Navigating through new technologies like Windows 11 comes with its fair share of challenges, and sometimes, finding the right help on forums or the built-in Help and Tips might not resolve all your queries. This is where contacting Microsoft Support can be particularly beneficial. They provide several channels to ensure you receive the necessary guidance for any issues you may encounter.

Understanding Different Support Options

Microsoft offers a variety of support mechanisms, tailored to cater to different problems — from simple usage questions to more complex technical issues.

1. Using Online Support

The first step in seeking help involves leveraging the extensive online resources Microsoft provides:

- **Support Website**: Visit the official Microsoft Support website. Here, you can use the search bar to type your issue or browse through the common topics covering aspects of all Microsoft products.
- **Virtual Agent**: Microsoft's website includes a virtual agent—a type of chatbot—that can handle basic inquiries. If your question is more complex, the virtual agent can connect you to a live person.
- **Support Page for Windows 11**: Here you will find all information specifically tailored for Windows 11, from setup and installation to troubleshooting and recovery options.

2. Telephone Support

For those who prefer speaking with a support representative, Microsoft provides telephone support:

- **Find the Right Number**: Visit the Microsoft Support website and navigate to the contact section to find the telephone number for your region. They have specific lines for different regions and services.
- **Prepare Your Information**: Before you call, make sure you have all necessary information handy, such as your Windows version, details of any error messages, and a brief explanation of the issue.
- **Be Patient**: Wait times can vary, so it's important to call when you have sufficient time to explain your issue and walk through any solutions with the support agent.

3. Email Support

If your issue isn't urgent, email support can be a good option:

- **Access Through the Support Site**: Navigate to the Microsoft Support site and choose the email option. You'll be prompted to fill in details about your issue.
- **Detail Your Problem**: When writing your email, provide as much detail as possible—screenshots of the issue can be particularly helpful.
- **Check Your Inbox**: Keep an eye on your email for a response. Microsoft typically provides timely replies, depending on the complexity of the issue.

4. Microsoft Store Support

If you live near a Microsoft Store, you can also seek face-to-face support:

- **In-person Help**: Visit your local Microsoft Store and talk to a technician. This can be ideal for hardware-related issues with your device.
- **Schedule an Appointment**: To avoid waiting, it's advisable to schedule an appointment online through the Microsoft Store website before your visit.

Best Practices When Contacting Support

To ensure a smooth support experience, here are some tips:

- **Be Prepared**: Before contacting support, gather all the necessary information about your problem, including software version, device types, and any steps you have already tried.

- **Describe Clearly**: When explaining your issue, be as clear and concise as possible. This helps the support agent understand your problem more quickly and provide accurate solutions.

- **Follow Instructions**: During the support session, carefully follow all guidance provided by the support agent. If something isn't clear, don't hesitate to ask for clarification.

Leveraging Accessibility Support

Microsoft is committed to accessibility, ensuring all users can effectively use their products:

- **Accessibility Desk**: Microsoft offers a dedicated support line for customers with disabilities. Here, specially trained agents are available to assist with accessibility features and related issues.

- **Using Accessibility Resources**: Microsoft's website includes a section dedicated to accessibility resources, offering guides and how-to articles on using accessibility features built into Windows 11.

Conclusion

Whether you're facing a minor hiccup or a major hurdle with Windows 11, remember that help is only a contact away. Microsoft's support services are designed to ensure you receive the assistance you need. By utilizing these support channels effectively, you can enhance your experience and continue enjoying the new features of Windows 11 with confidence. Remember, every query you resolve adds to your knowledge and makes you more adept at navigating this modern operating system.

HELPFUL RESOURCES AND TUTORIALS

In this digital age, mastering new software like Windows 11 can seem daunting, especially without the right guidance. Fortunately, there are numerous helpful resources and tutorials available at your disposal, designed to simplify your learning process. These tools are particularly beneficial in understanding the nuances of Windows 11, helping you to use your computer more effectively and efficiently.

Online Video Tutorials

One of the most accessible ways to learn new features of Windows 11 is through online video tutorials. These videos often provide step-by-step visual guides that are easy to follow.

1. **YouTube**: Platforms like YouTube have myriad channels dedicated to technology tips. Channels such as TechGumbo or Briteco9 offer detailed tutorials catering to both beginners and advanced users.

2. **Microsoft's Official YouTube Channel**: Don't forget to check out the official Microsoft Windows YouTube channel, which often posts helpful videos on the latest updates and features.

Written Guides and Articles

If you prefer reading at your own pace, numerous websites and blogs detail every aspect of Windows 11.

1. **Microsoft's Support Page**: Microsoft's own website has comprehensive guides on every feature within Windows 11, ensuring you get information straight from the source.

2. **Tech Blogs**: Websites like How-To Geek, CNET, and PCMag commonly publish easy-to-read articles and guides on various aspects of using Windows 11.

eBooks and Manuals

For a more thorough approach, eBooks and downloadable manuals can be a rich resource.

1. **Microsoft's Downloadable Resources**: Microsoft offers free downloadable PDF guides for Windows 11 that can be accessed directly from their support page.
2. **Online Book Retailers**: Websites like Amazon or Barnes & Noble offer eBooks that cover extensive topics on Windows 11, often updated with the latest features.

Interactive Webinars and Courses

Joining webinars and online courses can also significantly enhance your understanding by providing interactive learning experiences.

1. **Microsoft Events**: Keep an eye on upcoming webinars and virtual events hosted by Microsoft. These are especially useful for understanding updates or new features.
2. **Online Learning Platforms**: Sites like Udemy, Coursera, and LinkedIn Learning offer courses on Windows 11, often structured for users at different proficiency levels.

Community Help and Forums

Apart from professional resources, community help forums are invaluable for real-time assistance and shared knowledge from other users.

1. **Microsoft Community Forum**: This is a platform where you can ask questions, share experiences, and learn from other Windows users.
2. **Reddit and Quora**: These websites feature communities like r/windows and topics on Quora where users discuss tips, tricks, and troubleshoot together.

Local Workshops and Classes - If you prefer in-person learning, check out local resources:

1. **Community Centers or Libraries**: Often, these institutions hold free or low-cost classes on basic computer skills and how to use Windows 11.
2. **Tech Stores**: Some technology stores offer workshops which can be beneficial for hands-on learning experiences.

Tips for Utilizing These Resources - To make the most out of these resources, here are some strategies:

1. **Follow Along**: If using video tutorials or webinars, try to follow along on your own device. This hands-on practice can help solidify your learning.
2. **Take Notes**: Keeping notes, whether digital or on paper, can help you remember steps and procedures for later use.
3. **Bookmark and Save**: Bookmark pages, save tutorials, and organize links in a way that makes them easy to find when you need them.

Regular Updates and Continuous Learning - Windows 11, like all technology, evolves through updates and new features. Keeping up with these changes is crucial:

1. **Subscribe to Newsletters**: Tech websites and Microsoft often offer newsletters that keep you updated on the latest software changes and tips.
2. **Regular Review**: Periodically revisit your favorite resources to see what's new or any additional insights they might offer.

Conclusion - Using Windows 11 doesn't have to be an overwhelming journey. With an abundance of resources at your fingertips—from videos and tutorials to interactive courses and community forums—you can navigate and master Windows 11 at your own pace. Remember, the key to learning new technology is patience and persistence. Use these resources as a stepping stone to becoming proficient with your computer and embrace the process of continuous learning.